Literary Contexts

Postmodern Literatures

Literary Contexts recognises that literature is always rooted in its social milieu and that we need to study literary cultures in all their complexity and connections. It offers the thrill of locating a text within its context and seeing a context reflected in a literary/cultural text.

Each of the books in the series offers students of English and other literatures concise, informative insights into the history of ideas embodied in literary texts, authors and movements. Organised around themes and ideas with extensive examples from literary and cultural texts, the books enable students to understand how the "literary" takes shape in an intellectual milieu and discover manifestations of abstract ideas in literary texts. Written by scholar-teachers who have taught and researched literature for several years, each volume in the series is a stand-alone reference book for students and teachers alike.

Series editor

Pramod K. Nayar teaches at the Department of English, University of Hyderabad. His most recent books include *Bhopal's Ecological Gothic: Disaster, Precarity and the Biopolitical Uncanny* (2017), *The British Raj: Keywords* (2017), *Human Rights and Literature: Writing Rights* (2016) and *The Indian Graphic Novel: Nation, History and Critique* (2016).

Also in the series

Shakespeare
American Literature
Modern English Literature, 1890–1960
Victorian Literature
Postcolonial Literatures
Eighteenth-century English Literature
English Romantic Literature

LITERARY CONTEXTS

Postmodern Literatures

Avishek Parui

Series Editor
Pramod K. Nayar

Orient BlackSwan

POSTMODERN LITERATURES

ORIENT BLACKSWAN PRIVATE LIMITED

Registered Office
3-6-752 Himayatnagar, Hyderabad 500 029, Telangana, India
e-mail: centraloffice@orientblackswan.com

Other Offices
Bengaluru, Bhopal, Chennai, Guwahati, Hyderabad, Jaipur, Kolkata, Lucknow, Mumbai, New Delhi, Noida, Patna, Vijayawada

First published 2018

028416

ISBN 978 93 5287 463 7

Typeset in Adobe Caslon Pro 11.5/14.3 *by*
Akhil Offset Printers
Hyderabad 500 020

Printed and bound at
Graphica Printers & Binders, Hyderabad 500 013

Published by
Orient Blackswan Private Limited
3-6-752, Himayatnagar, Hyderabad 500 029
e-mail: hyderabad@orientblackswan.com

Contents

Series Editor's Preface

The idea that the literature of every age is rooted in its social milieu is a truism. Mapping the contours of this milieu often requires, for the student, to read through several specialised texts. Titles in *Literary Contexts*, by bringing together the key contexts – both general and specialised – into one volume, offer the student of English and other literatures short, prescient and informative studies that provide the history of ideas embodied in literary texts, authors and movements.

Intellectual history or the history of ideas has always been intertwined with the cultural practices and shifts within them in every age. Therefore titles in the series track the intellectual history of every age through social and historical contexts, whether these were contexts of imperial voyages, "Westward expansion", the Reformation of the Church, great scientific discoveries or nationalist movements. Considerable attention is paid to the contexts of class, literacy, gender relations, the state and its functions in every age.

The series' titles demonstrate how certain dominant ideas in any age operated. To this end, every title in the series draws upon and cites numerous examples from literary texts. This enables the student to get a sense of the literary themes' origins in the intellectual milieu, and discover manifestations of abstract ideas, such as "exceptionalism", "hybrid and displaced identity" or "division of powers of Church and State", in literary texts.

The authors do not seek to establish a direct correspondence between the literary text and the dominant idea of the age, but they off er the student a sense of the dense exchanges between the idea and the literary text. Each title maps ideas across cultural texts – popular forms, high culture, and scientific and philosophical texts – so that it demonstrates how ideas are mobile and cut across genres and domains. The titles in the series also document the conflicts and tensions in every age so that the student is made aware of the complicated nature of both, the history of ideas and the literary expressions of the same, and is alerted to the messy nature of cultural history of any age, in any nation.

This volume departs from the series in some significant ways. Focusing mainly upon textual manifestations of contexts – cultural, political, economic – the volume tracks them back into the congeries of ideas, movements and intellectual trends. Textual analysis is treated as a methodological tool to unpack the contexts embedded in them, rather than use the contexts as frames within which to read texts. This may make the particular volume challenging, but it may also be understood as a typical postmodern move where figure and ground are reversed constantly.

Written by scholar-teachers who have taught and researched literature for several years, *Literary Contexts* is student-friendly, being both jargon-free and incisive.

Pramod K. Nayar

Acknowledgements

When Pramod Nayar first proposed that I write the book on Postmodern Literature as part of the Literary Contexts series published by Orient BlackSwan, of which he is the general editor, I was simultaneously thrilled and daunted. Thrilled because postmodern literature has always been one of my natural interests as a student. Daunted because this meant writing an entire book on a subject that is fiercely contested and debated upon. This work is a modest attempt at a renewed articulation of the significance of postmodernism and postmodernist literature in the context of our times. Although I have enjoyed the writing process immensely, it was a challenge to situate the selected texts and their contexts into a postmodernist narrative of enquiry that informs one book. For postmodernism is notorious in its debunking of any attempt to forge a master narrative and I have often wondered if writing a book on postmodernism is like a self-defeating exercise. Of course it is. Of course it isn't.

I have extensively drawn on the many conversations and discussions I have been very fortunate to enjoy with a number of scholars. Special thanks to Patricia Waugh who supervised my PhD at Durham University. It's always a special delight and honour to quote and cite someone one has academically as well as informally known and shared stories with. As one of the key figures in the study of postmodernist literature and metafiction, Pat's significance in the context of this book is towering and telling. Thanks to Ankhi Mukherjee, Jason Harding and Simon James for their constant and very generous academic support over the years. I am very grateful to the general editor of this series and my good friend Pramod Nayar, to Sreenath S from Orient BlackSwan for trusting me with this work, and to Ishita Chatterji for her careful and excellent editing of my drafts.

My final and fullest note of gratitude goes to my wife Priyanka, who has always been my first and finest reader, with her special gifts and consistent commitment to everything honest, creative and constructive.

I dedicate my first book to Priyanka and to our son, Ayanish, who happens to share his birthday with James Joyce.

INTRODUCTION

Postmodernism in literature is most commonly classified as, among other things, the period of literary production post–Second World War. This commonly accepted description is, however, immediately fraught with contingencies, contradictions and confusions, states which ironically corroborate[1] the stylistic features of postmodern literature and literary aesthetics. For to define the postmodern in a strictly temporal sense would be to immediately exclude a plethora of literary styles and works that would otherwise qualify as benchmarks of high–postmodernist writing. The list of scandalous exclusions would include – but would definitely not be limited to – François Rabelais's *Gargantua and Pantagruel* (1693–94), Miguel de Cervantes's *Don Quixote* (1615), Laurence Sterne's *Tristram Shandy* (1759), Jonathan Swift's *A Modest Proposal* (1729), Oscar Wilde's *The Importance of Being Earnest* (1895) as well as James Joyce's *Finnegans Wake*, a novel published on 4 May 1939, four months before the start of the Second World War.

As in most other "post"-isms, postmodernism in literature straddles calendar time as well as textual strategies, historical space as well as stylistic subversions. However, its embeddedness in a *permanent prolepsis* – the fact that it is suggestive of a state always *after* what is "modern" or "now" – invests an impossibility of definition and containment that has come to characterise postmodernist writing. This impossibility finds its aesthetic ally in the postmodernist avant-garde[2] that permanently problematises any division between high and low culture, tribute and parody, seriousness and flippancy. The postmodern in literature may thus be best described as an entanglement,[3] an aesthetic of anti-authoritarianism and permanent polyphony that characterises the works of Rabelais as well as Rushdie, Kafka as well as Calvino, Cervantes as well as Spiegelman. In keeping with an aesthetic of entanglement – a term borrowed from quantum theory – postmodernism eschews hierarchy in favour of *heterarchy* – a term borrowed from computer science and popularised by the computer scientist Warren McCulloch and subsequently by cognitive theorist Douglas Hofstadter. The *heterarchical* order of postmodernist fiction, whereby the narrative often operates like a distributive chain, directly informs the postmodernist poetics of polyphony and centrelessness. In such poetics, characters and events often appear as projections and possibilities rather than certainties and realities. The salient features of postmodernist fiction may be listed as follows:

- a self-reflexive, self-conscious metafictional aesthetic with an awareness of its own constructed quality
- a resistance against and a retelling of all grand and totalitarian narratives of nation, history, identity and culture
- a promotion of the playful and the problematic that interrogates the profundity informing the politics of presuppositions
- a proclivity towards textuality and narrativity: transforming time, space, identity and history into texts and narratives that can be constructed as well as deconstructed
- an economy of intersubjective intertextuality that is tied to the metafictional quality of the narrative, whereby the fictional text strategically refers to, draws on, imitates, pays tribute to, parodies and generates mutable meanings out of other fictional texts surreptitiously as well as explicitly

What is immediately revealed in the indicative (but by no means exhaustive) list of features above is a sense of polyphonic praxis that characterises the postmodern problematic where the high and the low, the real and the fictional, the organic and the inorganic, are all endlessly enmeshed. More importantly, and at a stylistic level, postmodernism eschews descriptions and "self-referential transparency" in favour of an endless self-reflexivity whereby it describes just itself as well as its "non-identity with itself" (Derrida, *Acts of Literature* 211). Instead of objectivity and facticity, postmodernist poetics relies more on unreliability and plasticity as stylistic and thematic categories, in an ironic optimisation of its ontology. In emerging as the dynamic in which "the modern puts forward the unpresentable in presentation itself", postmodernism denies itself "the solace of good forms, the consensus of a taste which would make it possible to share collectively the nostalgia for the unattainable" (Lyotard 81), even as it questions its own epistemological process. As a problematic of presuppositions and essence, postmodernism subjects itself to its own critical tools and creative strategies in an inescapable loop of self-reflexivity and self-critique. Designed to direct itself against totalising narratives of seamless continuity that demand to be reckoned as metaphysical, metadiscursive givens, postmodernist poetics becomes a celebration of simultaneity, interruption, incompletion and incongruity.

Metafiction, or a fictional narrative acutely and aesthetically aware of its own constructed quality, is one of the core components of postmodernist poetics. The self-consciousness of the metafictional narrative lends itself to the self-critique of postmodernist poetics. From John Fowles's *The French Lieutenant's Woman* (1969) to John Barth's *Lost in the Funhouse* (1968), from Italo Calvino's *If on a Winter's Night a Traveller* (1979) to Salman Rushdie's *Midnight's Children* (1981), the metafictional quality whereby the narrative proceeds through a process of self-conscious storytelling is an immediate instantiation of postmodernist fiction. The characters in the metafictional postmodernist novel thus emerge as *hyperfictionalised* entities tied to the text and the discourse that produces it. Thus, the figures in Maggie Gee's metafictional murder mystery *Dying, In Other Words* (1981) are acutely aware of and articulate their locations as characters in a fictional text, outside of which they do not exist. Likewise, the hero of Steve Katz's *The Exaggerations of Peter Prince* (1968) is unashamedly protected by the author, who designs a *deus ex machina* in order to ensure that his fictional protagonist and, by extension his plot, survive an untimely demise. Producing narcissistic narratives where characters are acutely aware of and constantly dramatise their fictionality, postmodernist metafiction breaks away from the structure of classic realism – which is equated with the bourgeois politics of production by theorists such as Donna Haraway, as will be examined subsequently – and "parodies and imitates as a way to a new form which is just as serious and valid, as a synthesis, as the form it dialectically attempts to surpass" (Hutcheon, *Narcissistic Narrative* 25). The metafictional quality embedded in the literary novel has made its presence felt since the novel's earliest days – as immediately evident in Sterne's *Tristram Shandy* and Cervantes's *Don Quixote* – but postmodernist poetics gives it a fresh and systematised lease in its attempt to articulate the constructed quality of meanings, narratives and identities (Waugh 84–85).[5]

The intertextuality[6] of the postmodernist narrative is premised on a hyperlink quality whereby the text falls back, draws on, and often revises earlier texts in an entanglement of acknowledgement and deliberate misappropriation. A classic case in point is J. M. Coetzee's novel *Foe* (1986), which is a retelling of Daniel Defoe's *Robinson Crusoe* (1719) from the standpoint of a female writer who seeks to situate not Crusoe but Man Friday as the storyteller. Coetzee's narrative is acutely aware of its fictional constructed quality apropos of the earlier work of fiction and thus appropriates a metafictional, intertextual character in its structure of storytelling. Likewise, John Gardner's *Grendel* (1971) retells the Beowulf story from the point of view of the monster and Jean Rhys's *Wide Sargasso Sea* (1966) is a prequel as well as a retelling of Charlotte Brontë's *Jane Eyre* (1847) from the point of view of Bertha Mason, who is the madwoman of the attic in Brontë's novel. The protagonist of Flann O'Brien's *At Swim-Two-Birds* (1939), commonly classified as one of the first postmodernist novels, articulates the aspiration of the modern storyteller to be endlessly intertextual, stating that characters "should be interchangeable as between one book and another. The entire corpus of existing literature should be regarded as a limbo from which discerning authors could draw their characters as required, creating only when they failed to find a suitable existing puppet. The modern novel should be largely a work of reference" (25).

With its special and revisionary attention to the textuality of thought and practices, postmodernism offers a unique insight into history and shared symbolic systems. Far from being ahistorical or insensitive to cultural codes, postmodernism emerges as an *aesthetic and cultural condition* that constantly questions even as it playfully opens up the borderlines between the imaginary and the symbolic, thus extending onto alliances with history, philosophy, psychology, mathematics, computer science and cybernetics, along with other networks of knowledge.[7] Minimalist as well as excessive, constative as well as performative, stylised as well as subversive, postmodernist poetics thus becomes "fundamentally contradictory, resolutely historical and inescapably political" (Hutcheon, *A Poetics of Postmodernism* 4) in its play between referentiality and non-referentiality. With its "incredulity toward metanarratives" (Lyotard xxiv), postmodernism invests attention in the very politics of meaning formation, and with its metafictional narrative aesthetics, it often enacts an endless process of frame-breaking which blurs the borderlines between the real and the fictional while dramatising an order of "superrealism" (McHale 197) that unsettles the ontology of occurrence. As Thanatz in

Thomas Pynchon's *Gravity's Rainbow* realises, "[o]f course it happened. Of course it didn't happen" (788).

Philosophical and Critical Currents in Postmodernism

Despite the temporal contingencies surrounding the term postmodern, it is possible to trace a genealogy and a historical overview of the same. Coined by Arnold Toynbee in 1939 as a temporal definition of the post–1914 world, the term postmodern was first used as a metaphor for design in 1945 by Joseph Hudnut who used the word to describe new architectural achievements.[8] What the year 1922 was to English literary modernism – the year that saw the emergence of James Joyce's *Ulysses*, Virginia Woolf's *Mrs. Dalloway* and T. S. Eliot's *The Waste Land* – could be said about the year 1939 apropos of postmodernism. For 1939 was the year which saw the publication of Joyce's *Finnegans Wake*, Nathalie Sarraute's *Tropismes* and Flann O'Brien's *At Swim-Two-Birds*, texts that deliberately defamiliarise the difference between event and non-event, remembering and storytelling, with their playful metafictional aesthetics. The language games, paralogy, ephemeral temporality, non-referentiality, nihilism of knowledge, states that characterise the postmodern condition, all find their early and systematic representations in these literary works, only to be further accentuated by more systematised literary movements such as the Theatre of the Absurd and Magic Realism as well as in critical theories such as post-structuralism and posthumanism.

A historical examination of postmodernism in literature and literary studies will be fuller and more faithful if it is undertaken along with a study of the philosophy and critical theory that informed the postmodernist turn. The historian of postmodernism – an identity informed as well as unsettled by irony, given the postmodernist proclivity to play with and problematise genres and definitions – could do worse than begin with Friedrich Nietzsche in order to examine the epistemology of counter-narratives that characterise postmodernist poetics. The Nietzschean genealogy of history appears to anticipate the postmodernist *historiographic metafiction*, a self-conscious, self-reflexive style of looking at history as an entanglement of macro and micro narratives, playfully problematised by creative insertions and unreliable fabulation. The blurring of borderlines between history and fiction is creatively captured by several postmodernist narratives including Günter Grass's *The Tin Drum* (1959), E. L. Doctorow's *Ragtime* (1975), Salman Rushdie's *Midnight's Children* (1981), Martin Amis's *Time's Arrow* (1991) and Thomas Pynchon's *Mason & Dixon* (1997). What distinguishes historiographic metafiction – a term introduced and popularised by Linda Hutcheon – is a deliberately defamiliarised entanglement of historical events and fictional episodes that are often represented in strategically stylised and self-reflexive storytelling. Historiographic metafiction attempts to unsettle the objective order of historical knowledge by weaving in fantasy and facticity in narrative networks that subvert standard notions of logic, identity, space and time. Far from being hedonistically ahistorical or escapist, historiographic metafiction offers an alternative understanding of history and historical knowledge by cracking open and playing with the epistemic politics in history-writing itself.

In many senses, Nietzsche could conveniently be classified as perhaps having been one of the first philosophers of the postmodern tradition, with his intellectual inquests into the death of God (God being symbolic of a semiological centre or an ontological origin) and the grand narratives of history, civilisation and monumentality. Nietzsche's project, most notably in *The Use and Abuse of History* originally written in 1873, to "bring the past to the bar of judgment, interrogate it remorselessly" (Nietzsche 20–21) clearly anticipates postmodernist historians such as Hayden White who seek to deconstruct the "conceptual apparatus" (White 30) that goes into the ordering of history and history writing. Like Paul Veyne, Michel de Certeau, Dominick LaCapra and Lionel Gossman, White challenges the seemingly non-narrative nature and the "ontological integrity" (Gay 210) of history as upheld by critics such as Peter Gay, and instead examines the figurative, fictive and allegorical quality of the historical narrative that is textualised and interpreted even during the act of formation. In this revisionist allegorical view of history, the borderlines between real history and historical fiction such as Grass's *The Tin Drum* and Rushdie's *Midnight's Children* become complex and contingent.

If Nietzsche may be regarded as one of the first philosophers of the postmodernist critique of the "metaphysics of essence"[9] (Thiher 195), the figure who is perhaps most historically significant in terms of examining the constructed quality and the ideologies informing identity, the politics of power and the *order of things* is Michel Foucault (1926–84). Foucault's early work – appearing largely in the early 1970s – is an examination of knowledge as embedded in an archaeological quality, stepping out, as do the works of Jacques Derrida, of the humanist universals of language and discourse. Describing *discursive practices* as "historical rules" that determine and are in turn determined by "social, economic, geographical or linguistic area" and emerge as an "enunciative function" (*The Archaeology of Knowledge* 119), Foucault appears to anticipate much of postmodernism's critical energies aimed against a totalitarian episteme of power and knowledge. Especially examining the politics of power production, Foucault defines the same as "the moving substrate of force relations" (*The History of Sexuality* 90) which generates inequality as well as permanence. It is this order of totalitarian permanence against which the postmodernist poetics of impermanence and change situates itself. It does so with an entanglement of irony and self-reflexivity (for postmodernism is careful to interrogate and unpack its own epistemological process) that aims to deconstruct the discursive disguises informing the master narratives of individual as well as shared identities in space and time. By dismantling and deconstructing the invisible strategies that produce, protect and perpetuate power relations, Foucault accentuates the postmodernist turn that appears in the middle of the twentieth century. He is one of the first philosophers to examine the discursivity of history and the historicity of discourse, defining the latter as a "unity and discontinuity in history itself" (*The Archaeology of Knowledge* 117). Foucault's decentring of the discourses of power and authority has a direct and immediate relevance to literary studies for it extends onto the decentring of the author and the authorial voice, perhaps most powerfully instantiated in his essay "What is an Author?" (1969), philosophically dialogic with Roland Barthes's more provocative "The Death of the Author" (1967).

The life and work of Roland Barthes (1915–80) is perhaps most emblematic of the critical theory aligned to postmodernist poetics. Writing about the symbolic significance of Einstein's brain in popular culture as well as about the face of Greta Garbo; about narrative strategy in Balzac's stories as well as about structural semiotics operative in wrestling matches, Barthes's oeuvre of critical production corresponds directly to the merge of the high and the low, the avant-garde and the kitsch, that characterises postmodernism as a literary and artistic activity. An early example of what Rosalind Krauss describes as the *paraliterary space*, one characterised by "quotation, partisanship, betrayal, reconciliation" (37) as opposed to resolution or unification, Barthes's commentary on literature, art and culture is a testimony to the *textuality* that characterises postmodernism and postmodernist poetics. His *Mythologies* (1957) is a remarkable revision of the discursive structures and sentiments that pass off as givens in cultural codes and epistemic exchanges. One of the finest commentaries on popular culture as well as ideological investments, *Mythologies* examines the visual grammar of striptease as well as steak and chips, myth as a semiological system as well as the bourgeoisie as a joint stock company. A perfect specimen of the postmodernist critical energy, *Mythologies* is scandalous as well as scholastic, pop as well as profound, thus dramatising criticism as "a series of intellectual acts profoundly committed to the historical and subjective existence (they are the same) of the man who performs them" (Barthes, *Critical Essays* 257).

Quite literally, Barthes advocates a shift from *work* to *text*, defining the latter as "that social space which leaves no language safe, outside, nor any subject of the enunciation in position as judge, master, analyst, confessor, decoder" (*Image, Music, Text* 164). The constant contamination enacted by the text is testimony to the postmodernist poetics of resistance and revision. Starting as a structuralist, Barthes quickly moved onto a poststructuralist position where the play between the signifier (the sign) and the signified (meaning) is always mutable, moving and self-reflexive. Barthes takes the ontology of the text even further by making a distinction between *readerly* (listible) and *writerly* (scriptible) texts. While the former is irreversible and leaves no agency to the reader except to accept or reject it, the latter requires constant re-production on the part of the reader, and is thus reversible in its ontological status as text. One can see the immediate implication of this theory for postmodernist poetics, with novels such as John Fowles's *The French Lieutenant's Woman* (1969) and Martin Amis's *Time's Arrow* (1991) subscribing to the structure, sign and play of the Barthesian scriptible text that enacts a blissful violence on standard notions of space, storytelling and time. Barthes is most famous for his take on the death of the author – a position that may be seen as a philosophical extension of the Nietzschean death of God as an ontological origin – and his legacies on postmodernism and postmodernist poetics can hardly be overestimated. The essay

"The Death of the Author" (1967), with its historical study of the politics of authorship and its associated authority, has had direct and permanent impact on postmodernist poetics which constantly questions the ontology of the author through its self-reflexive metafictional aesthetics. This is evident in one of the very first and finest postmodernist novels – Flann O'Brien's *At Swim-Two-Birds* (1939), where the author of the inset-novel is tried by his characters for the injustices he had committed while creating them.[10] Barthes's autobiography – *Roland Barthes by Roland Barthes* (1975) – is a classic postmodernist text in itself with its play between fact and fabulation, remembering and storytelling, starting as it does with the assertion: "[i]t must all be considered as if spoken by a character in a novel" (i).

Postmodernism and Deconstruction

Perhaps the single most influential essay in a study of postmodernism, one that extends onto an endless critique of all metaphysics of essence, is Jacques Derrida's "Structure, Sign and Play in the Discourse of the Human Sciences", originally a lecture delivered at John Hopkins University in 1966. The Derridean *différance*, with its endless entanglement of differing and deferring, may be considered as one of the key concepts informing the postmodernist play between structure and sign, between sign and meaning. As Derrida himself explains, the "a" of *différance* "recalls that spacing is temporization, the detour and postponement by means of which intuition, perception, consummation – in a word, the relationship to the present, the reference to a present reality, to a *being* – are always *deferred*" (*Positions* 28–29, italics in original) .

The Derridean description of space and temporality as a complex that is endlessly slippery finds artistic resonance in many postmodernist novels such as Raymond Federman's *Take It or Leave It* (1976) which contains a provocative "Pretext" subtitled "a spatial displacement of words" that can be inserted anywhere in the body of the work. Inhabiting the realms of philosophy as well as literary theory, Derrida and his Deconstruction sent waves of new insights and inquests directed against some of the foundational principles of Western logic and metaphysics. Describing presuppositions as "parts of a pseudo-whole" ("Voice ii" 84), Derridean Deconstruction allied itself with post-structuralism and the "breaches or infractions" (*Positions* 69) it produced which in turn generated a permanent suspension and suspicion of ontological origins. Examining the endless ludic quality of meaning formation at the strictly semantic as well as at the broader cultural level, Deconstruction appropriates the "absence of the transcendental signified as non-limitation of the game" (Derrida, *Of Grammatology* 50). Examining what *happens* as also a *desire* that what *does not happen* should happen, and thus a story that entangles the archive of the real with the archive of the fictional (*Acts of Literature* 35), Derrida opens up the possibilities of literature becoming a profoundly political act.

Most significantly for postmodernist literature, Derrida examines the non-innocence of metaphors, "the animality of the letter" (*Writing and Difference* 88–89) and the figurative quality of philosophy itself as a form of self-reflexive language. Derrida's intellectual inquests into the works of James Joyce are well known. He defines *Finnegans Wake* as a text that forms, fuses and forges a heteroglossia of history, myths and narratives. In doing so, it foregrounds its own forgery, and in the camouflage of coined words, produces an unreliable mosaic of memory. Derrida's descriptions of Joyce's 1939 novel may be read as the formative principle of a classic-postmodernist text:

> He repeats and mobilizes and babelizes the (asymptotic) totality of the equivocal, he makes this his theme and his operation, he tries to make outcrop, with the greatest possible synchrony, at great speed, the greatest power of the meanings buried in each syllabic fragment, subjecting each atom of writing to fission in

> order to overload the unconscious with the whole memory of man: mythologies, religion, philosophies, sciences, psychoanalysis, literatures. ("Two Words for Joyce" 149)

Derrida's Deconstruction does not seek to destroy meanings and their context, although it is often erroneously understood that way, like so much of postmodernist poetics. Instead, it opens up the possibilities of meaning and meaning-formation in texts and produces a critical current "possible only in a historical, political, theoretical, etc., situation that is highly determined" (*Positions* 63). In doing so, it subverts and permanently problematises the phallogocentrism that had historically informed white Western mythologies[11] of power and knowledge.

The works of Nietzsche, Foucault, Barthes and Derrida reveal a fundamental critique of the discursive which disguises as the universal. Examining the constructed quality of the structure, sign and play of language, discourse and power, these philosophers question the epistemological politics of epistemology itself and thus leave the legacy of a self-reflexive quality on postmodernist poetics that revises itself ad infinitum. Significantly, for literary writing, this ushered in a view of language which ceased to be a passive and objective reflection of an objective world and instead emerged as an "independent self-contained system which generates its own 'meanings'", appropriating a metafictional quality complexly connecting and exploring the "relationship between the world *of* the fiction and the world *outside* the fiction" (Waugh, *Metafiction* 3, italics in original).[12] The self-consciousness of the metafictional language of postmodernism extends from a *celebration of certaintylessness* that is ontologically different from uncertainty. Thus, while uncertainty entails a possibility and an inherent desire to achieve certainty either through discursive practices or fictional retellings, certaintylessness entails a state of permanent chaos which is not necessarily undesirable. The contrast between modernist and postmodernist fiction dramatises this difference.

Thus, while the myths in Eliot's *The Waste Land* or Joyce's *Ulysses*[13] look back nostalgically to a sense of pure past and lament its loss, the myths used in Rushdie's *Midnight's Children* take up a carnivalesque[14] quality that becomes a celebration of centrelessness which extends onto a euphoria of lost origins. As Andreas Huyssen argues in his influential essay on the various trajectories of postmodernism, it is perhaps best to see the postmodern turn as a continuation as well as a departure from modernism, rather than a pure extension or rupture, for "the question of historical continuity or discontinuity simply cannot be adequately discussed in terms of such an either/or dichotomy", the critique of which Huyssen attributes to the lasting legacy of Derridean Deconstruction (10).

Instead of the Kantian critique of pure reason, postmodernism offers a self-reflexive critique of cynical reason which relies more on "satirical intelligence" that "resembles literature more than systematized knowledge" in its endeavour to "disclose the questionable and ridiculous aspects of the grand, serious systems" (Sloterdijk 287–88).[15] More importantly, postmodernism is acutely aware of its own tendencies towards commodification, of becoming a grand narrative in itself in alliance with the logic of late capitalism, as argued by postmodernism's detractors such as Fredric Jameson who views postmodernism as being complicit and collusive with the consumerist culture and describes the self-referentiality of postmodernist art as a "pathology" that jeopardises the "position of the artist" ("In the Destructive Element Immerse" 103). In a more famous work, Jameson equates postmodernism with the cultural logic of late capitalism and argues that while modernism made an effort to critique or transcend commodification, "[p]ostmodernism is the consumption of sheer commodification as a process" (*Postmodernism* x). Examining how aesthetic production in postmodernism emerges "integrated with commodity production" (*Postmodernism* 10),[16] Jameson highlights what he describes as domestication of experimentation in a postmodern consumer culture, one which moves away from the modernist critique of kitsch and commodity.

However, it is precisely in its play between collusion and critique that postmodernism achieves its ontological complexity as an artistic strategy. Inescapably a part of the produce and purchase economy that characterises academia and high-critical theory in an age of digital reproduction – as the Marxist critic Theodor Adorno states, "[n]o theory today escapes the marketplace" (4) – postmodernist texts resist reification through self-reflexivity and self-critique through which they "foreground their own contradictions" (Hutcheon, *A Poetics of Postmodernism* 211). The strategically narcissistic narrative structures, self-awareness, sly civility, artificiality, mimicry, evasion with closures and the aesthetics of unreliability that characterise postmodernist poetics are essentially performative. As the theatre of Bertolt Brecht highlights, such performativity dramatises the myth of closure and continuity, and promotes an aesthetic of instability whereby the receiver shifts from "general passive acceptance to a corresponding state of suspicious inquiry" (Brecht 192).

Postmodernism as a Critique of Western Enlightenment Logic

The one common thread that connects almost all the thinkers and philosophers of the postmodernist tradition is a critique of the European and Eurocentric Enlightenment, a critique that lends itself richly to the counter-discourses informing postcolonial theory, feminism and posthumanism, among other critical currents. Beginning with the Nietzschean interrogation of ontological origins, through Foucauldian examinations of the architecture of power and Derridean studies of animality deconstructing the pure humanness of the Cartesian cogito,[17] right down to Lyotard's attack against grand narratives and Baudrillard's celebration of the simulacra, postmodernism has always been aimed against a totalitarian and exclusionist episteme of power and meaning production. Its critique of the metaphysics of meaning and the ontology of origins often extends onto a critique of knowledge that assumes totalitarian quality. As Andreas Huyssen argues, "postmodernism's critical dimension lies precisely in its radical questioning of those presuppositions which linked modernism and the avantgarde to the mindset of modernization" (11).

This postmodernist cynical critique operates at ideational as well as at political levels, mostly blurring the borderlines between the two. This is manifested in Jean-François Lyotard's description of the postmodernist artist:

> A postmodern artist or writer is in the position of a philosopher: the text he writes, the work he produces are not in principle governed by preestablished rules, and they cannot be judged according to a determining judgement, by applying familiar categories to the text or to the work. Those rules and categories are what the work of art itself is looking for. (81)

The *epistemological liminality* as described by Lyotard points to the postmodernist proclivity towards prolepsis, whereby *structures succeed signs* and not the other way around. This tendency towards non-referentiality as well as hyper-referentiality, sometimes simultaneously, characterises postmodernist imagination and is naturally allied with cynicism and ambivalence constantly questioning hegemonic knowledge at intellectual as well as political levels. This is reflected in the works of Jean Baudrillard (1929–2007) which offer a systematic cynicism directed against totalitarian narratives of consumer culture. Baudrillard's study of the simulacra as a play between reality and hyperreality, between facticity and fantasy, extends onto subversive readings of major political events such as the Gulf War and 9/11. Baudrillard defines postmodernist culture as a state of permanently playful Disneyland, where the artificial becomes the hyperreal through an increasing internalisation of immersive technology. His observations are particularly directed against the discursively mediated media that operates on simulation, pre-inscribed "orchestrated rituals" which "function as a set of signs dedicated exclusively to their recurrence as signs and no longer to their 'real' goal at all" (41).

Breaking off from the Hegelian dialectic of enlightenment, postmodernism inherits instead a self-reflexive negative dialectic, one that eschews immanence and instead generates a critical reflection of its own context, "reflects its own motion" (Adorno 141). In his provocatively postmodern essay entitled "The Animal That Therefore I Am", Derrida interrogates the Cartesian code of the immanent thinking self and the exclusive prestige associated with the same. Drawing on the poetics of Lewis Carroll's writing, Derrida deconstructs the human/animal binary that had informed Cartesian Enlightenment. In Derrida's playful pursuit, the borders between the organic and the inorganic become slippery and largely indeterminable. Examining what lies beyond the anthropocentric order of being and language, Derrida discovers "a heterogeneous multiplicity of the living . . . a multiplicity of organizations of relations between living and dead" (399). The Derridean critique of Enlightenment is extended onto the works of subsequent thinkers such as Gilles Deleuze, Félix Guattari and Donna Haraway who are instrumental in exploring the epistemic shift from humanism to posthumanism. Spiritually allied to the aesthetics of postmodernism, posthumanism questions the very binaries between man and machine, between the organic and the inorganic, investigating how the orders entangle in generating new networks of knowledge.

Unsurprisingly, this has immediate relevance and resonance with the postmodernist politics of narrative and narrativity. Thus, while Haraway offers the ontology of the cyborg – a creature simultaneously animal and machine – which explores and celebrates "transgressed boundaries, potent fusions and dangerous possibilities" (154) in its post-gender, post-Oedipal narrative, she also locates the same in the postmodernist plane of literary representation, as opposed to what she classifies as the realism of the bourgeois novel (161).[18] Examining Octavia Butler's *Dawn* (1987) – the first of her *Xenogenesis* trilogy (1987–2000) – as a "novel that interrogates reproductive, linguistic, and nuclear politics in a mythic field structured by late twentieth-century race and gender" (180), Haraway highlights some of the salient features of postmodernist poetics. Like the playful monstrosity of Haraway's cyborg, postmodernism entails a critique of totalising theories and master narratives of race and gender identities. This is achieved, not through "common language" but through "a powerful infidel heteroglossia" that subverts a shared sense of "holistic politics" (181).

If Haraway situates the cyborg as a postmodernist post-gender resistance to the heteronormative politics of production, the works of Gilles Deleuze and Felix Guattari examine the endless entanglement of knowledge-formation and dissemination in the postmodernist discourse network that is performative, plastic and proleptic. In remarkable resonance with Haraway's description of the cyborg as the postmodernist post-Oedipal entity, Deleuze and Guattari define the *rhizome* as that structural principle which "ceaselessly establishes connections between semiotic chains, organizations of power, and circumstances relative to the arts, sciences, and social struggles" (7). The rhizome is also characterised by disconnection, deterritorialisation, multiplicity and plasticity which Deleuze and Guattari discover in Noam Chomsky's syntagmatic model in linguistics, Franz Kafka's novels (where bureaucracy bludgeons by felling rhizomatic stems) and the city of Amsterdam, a city without roots and with stem-canals "where utility connects with the greatest folly in relation to a commercial war machine" (15). Speaking of short-term and long-term memory as rhizomatic and non-rhizomatic functions respectively, Deleuze and Guattari define the rhizome as an "interbeing, *intermezzo*", tracing the patterns in postmodern literature that "manifest this rhizomatic direction" as they seek to "move between things, establish a logic of the AND, overthrow ontology, do away with foundations, nullify endings and beginnings" (25, italics in original). A powerful and permanent break from the logos of Enlightenment, Deleuze describes an order of literary writing that appropriates the aesthetics of the *antilogos* where signs begin to speak for themselves, "reduced to the resources of disaster and deception" (Deleuze 113) and functioning without external referentiality or analogical grids.

As a critique of essence and Enlightenment, postmodernism inherits and extends a rich range of thoughts and thinkers from Derrida to Deleuze who are connected in their anti-foundational take on epistemology and epistemological narratives. Situating metafiction against metaphysics, artificiality against organicity, heterarchy against hierarchy, postmodernism and postmodernist poetics push the possibilities of articulation and representation, in a subversion of standard notions of space, cognition, identity and time. Appropriating the jolly relativity of Rabelais as well as the quantum relativity of Einstein, postmodernism may best be defined as an *endless activity of approximation and re-presentation* that keeps drawing attention to its own inorganicity and incompletion embedded within its aesthetics. This is immediately evident in postmodernist fictions – the multiverse of magic realism and metaphoric miniaturisation – that dramatise the disruptive, ludic and fictive qualities of embodiment, remembering and storytelling. In the process these expose and deconstruct the constructed quality of classic realism and instead offer a self-reflexive order of hypertextuality and hyperfictionality that highlights the ontological tension between "tropological reality and 'literal' reality" (McHale 146).

KEY TEXTS AND TEXTUAL STRATEGIES

In his work on the postmodern condition as a report of knowledge, Jean-François Lyotard describes the works of Marcel Proust and James Joyce as both alluding to an order of representation that is unrepresentable in the context of the present. However, while in Proust the unrepresentable subsumes the identity of the character's consciousness which becomes a labyrinth of time, in Joyce the very act of writing is opened up whereby the grammar and ritual of writing, especially literary writing, is no longer a given. Lyotard's study of the difference between Proust and Joyce is an examination of the difference between modernist and postmodernist writing. Thus, while modernist aesthetics emerges as a nostalgia of the sublime whereby the unrepresentable, although alluded to through the missing content, does not affect the narrative form, the case for the postmodernist writer or artist is distinctly different:

> The [postmodern] artist and the writer, then, are working without rules in order to formulate the rules of what *will have been done*. Hence the fact that work and text have the characteristics of an *event*; hence also, they always come too late for their author, or, what amounts to the same thing, their being put into work, their realization (*mise en oeuvre*) always begin too soon. *Post modern* would have to be understood according to the paradox of the future (*post*) anterior (*modo*). (Lyotard 81, italics in original)

Lyotard's description of the dynamics of postmodernist writing corresponds to the definition of postmodernism as a state of *permanent prolepsis* as described above. What is more significant in Lyotard's study above though is the ontology of postmodernist writing and art as a self-constructive category. It connects interestingly to Derrida's study of Kafka's "Before the Law", a drama of "an interminable *différance*" and a story that is "perfectly ended and yet brutally, one could say primally, cut short, interrupted" (Derrida, *Acts of Literature* 204, italics in original). One can see the immediate political and ideological implications of such strategies of subversion and interruption, especially when they are directed against totalitarian narratives of control and communication. Instead of commonsensical meanings which correspond to dominant discursive strategies, postmodernist literature is more geared towards producing alternative realities as in John Fowles's 1965 novel *The Magus*, where the fictional world of Bourani has "second meanings hung in the air, ambiguities, unexpectedness" (85).

In moving from reality to textuality, manoeuvered by the metafictional poetics that informs it, postmodernist literature pays special attention to the discursive quality of language in constructing reality. This discursive quality was best concealed and controlled by realism in literature which operated mostly on principles of verisimilitude, principles against which postmodernist poetics situates itself essentially and aesthetically. This is evocatively and unequivocally asserted by Roland Barthes thus: "[t]hese facts of language were not perceptible as long as literature pretended to be a transparent expression of either objective calendar time or of psychological subjectivity . . . as long as literature maintained a totalitarian ideology of the referent, or more commonly speaking, as long as literature was 'realistic'" ("To Write: An Intransitive Verb?" 138).

By examining classic realism as a construct that conceals other constructs in language, Barthes articulates one of the fundamental principles in postmodernist poetics, the self-reflexivity that draws attention to the constructed quality of reality and its dominant representational mode. What distinguishes postmodernist literature in general is its resistance to generic classifications and locations. The metafictional and intertextual quality in postmodernist fiction opens up the divisions between high and low literature, originality and artifice, purity and pastiche. Thus, it is interesting to observe how metafiction informs so many seemingly different genres of writing, including romance (Margaret Drabble's *The Waterfall* [1969] and John Barth's *Sabbatical* [1982]), science fiction (Thomas Pynchon's *Gravity's Rainbow* [1973] and Kurt Vonnegut's *The Sirens of Titan* [1959]) and family saga (John Irving's *The World According to Garp* [1978] and Vladimir Nabokov's *Ada, or Ardor* [1969]). What further distinguishes these writers and works is the seamless blend of the experimental and the popular orders, a feature that appears in other works of creative expression in postmodernism such as music and cinema.

The postmodernist self-reflexivity and self-consciousness represents reality as an intertext, a form of fiction that is "woven into all" and "more valid" and which is designed to produce "worlds as real as, but other than the world that is. Or was" (Fowles, *The French Lieutenant's Woman* 86). By extension, it questions the borders between dreams and reality, embodiment and fantasy. This is dramatically represented in Jorge Luis Borges's 1975 short story 'The Other', where the author (Borges) appears as an old man who sits on a bench beside his younger self and concludes that the latter must have dreamt him up. Likewise, the speaker in John Barth's 1968 short story "Night-Sea Journey" describes his mad dreams as an "unimaginable embodiment" (12) of himself whereby language exceeds the control of the author and the text translates into reality. The fictionality and the dreamscapes in postmodernist literature ask crucial questions about the nature of knowledge, creative writing and epistemological certainty.

Clarence Major's 1975 novel *Reflex and Bone Structure* contains a remarkable scene where a character named Dale enters a room by opening a door after standing on the threshold for some time. The narrator–observer sits with aching elbows pressed against a dressing table, watches Dale stand at the door and *erases* Dale from the scene till he is an optical afterimage. After a few moments of liminal reconstruction, Dale appears in the scene again, opens the door again and this time he enters the room (20).

This scene from Major's novel exemplifies the ontological certaintylessness that characterises the postmodernist order of things. It corresponds to Jacques Derrida's Deconstructionist practice in *Of Grammatology* of placing certain verbal signs *sous rature*, under erasure: "le signe ~~est~~ cette ~~chose~~ mal nommée" (*De la grammatologie* 31), crossing out signs in a way that still makes them visible, whereby an object or an identity becomes less a stable signifier and more a play between presence and non-presence. This play of signs and identities of course extends onto a play between event and its absence, as exemplified earlier in this chapter in Thanatz's admission in Thomas Pynchon's *Gravity's Rainbow* of an event simultaneously happening and not happening. The ontological play between presence and absence runs throughout the postmodernist discourse. One can see early examples of this in the works of Borges and Beckett. Thus, while there is a systematic representation of self-erasure characterising the characters in Beckett's *The Unnamable* (1952), and a presentation of narrators who create characters to play with only to de-create them in the end in *Stories and Texts for Nothing* (1967), Borges, in *A Personal Anthology* (1961) constructs flickering liquid-images of Spanish landscapes as focalised through the mutable mind of the philosopher Averroës.

What the techniques of hyperreal, hyperfictional creations and de-creations in Major, Beckett and Borges offer is not just an ontic problematic of signs and significations but also a broader debate about the nature of historical and embodied identity. Thus, Steve Katz's *The Exaggerations of Peter Prince* describes its hero as a being without history, "pieced apart", as his "past erases itself like a disappearing wake" while the inset-novelist attempts to "grab hold of my self and finish this novel without characters" (162), the self being permanently plastic and a play between a sign and its absence. The historiographic significance of postmodernist metafiction has already been touched upon in this introduction and will be dealt with in more detail in subsequent chapters. But what the deliberately hollowed out, formally experimental narratives of postmodernist literature also corroborate is the endless emergence of storytelling and the storytelling voice. This is most famously exhibited in the opening and closing words of Joyce's *Finnegans Wake* which form a single sentence that loops back to the beginning of the story (the words being "A way a lone a last a loved a long the" and "riverrun, past Eve and Adam's, from swerve of shore to bend of bay"). It also appears in a more nakedly minimalist form in John Barth's short story from *Lost in the Funhouse*, appropriately titled "Frame-Tale": ("Once upon a time there was a story that began / once upon a time there was a story that began"). The infinite regress represented in such stylistic features may be traced back to the figure of Scheherazade in *One Thousand and One Nights* who used endless storytelling as a method of self-sustenance and survival. But the recursive quality, the nested loops, the inset-narratives, features that underline classic postmodernist texts such as John Fowles's *The French Lieutenant's Woman*, Gilbert Sorrentino's *Mulligan Stew* (1979) and Italo Calvino's *If on a Winter's Night a Traveller*, emerge not just as a stylistic category but an epistemic activity characterised by hyperreality, interruptions and auto-reversibility.

Unsurprisingly, the epistemic activity characterising postmodernist fiction as described above is also often underlined by a *trompe-l'oeil* quality whereby the reader is deliberately led down the garden path and tricked into events, figures and substances that may or may not exist. The Chinese-box *hypodiegetic* (narrative embedded within a narrative) structure of many postmodernist novels lends itself to the formal innovations as well as the deliberately unreliable and often mutually contradictory voices telling their stories. This generates what Jean Ricardou describes as "variable reality" whereby an apparently unreal, unreliable order of reality is revealed to be actually real in the end (23–43). A classic case in point is, again, Pynchon's *Gravity's Rainbow* where the entire story is retrospectively revealed as a cinema within the novel's central narrative frame: "[t]he screen is a dim page spread before us, white and silent. The film has broken, or a projector bulb has burned out. It was difficult even for us, old fans who've always been at the movies (haven't we?) to tell which before the darkness swept in" (760).

Blending in the novel's narrative with the film's diegesis, *Gravity's Rainbow* highlights storytelling as a medium in itself, pointing to a permanently playful and unreliable voice designed to generate distrust and deception rather than comfort and closure. Unlike the unreliable storyteller in Joseph Conrad's novel, the postmodernist order of narrative unreliability as exemplified by Pynchon is not melancholic or nostalgic, longing for an organic ontological origin that is now lost. Instead what often emerges in the postmodernist narrative cosmos is an example of *metalepsis*, or a looping back and across time and events, something Douglas Hofstadter describes as "strange loop phenomenon", a "tangled hierarchy" where "we unexpectedly find ourselves right back where we started" (10). Examples of metaleptic narratives are abundantly available in postmodernist fiction, from Christine Brooke-Rose's *Thru* (1975) where multiple levels of narration happen simultaneously and it is impossible to determine which level is diegetically superior to the other, to Fowles's *The French Lieutenant's Woman* (a text that will be examined in detail later in this book) where the narrated story and the narrating voice are endlessly entangled.

As the subsequent chapters will show, postmodernist fiction is essentially an opening up of the ontology of *givenness*, whereby the reified relationships between author and character, time and space, history and identity, substance and its absence, are debunked and deconstructed. Thus, texts such as *Midnight's Children*, *Invisible Cities*, *Time's Arrow*, *Foe* and *The Tin Drum* reveal contested terrains of identity-formation through a mutable medium that endlessly draws attention to itself. The metafictionality, plasticity, intertextuality, hyperreality and unreliability that characterise postmodernist poetics find their manifestations not just in literature and literary works but also in cinema, music and advertisements, which emerge as texts in popular culture. Often in alliance with the philosophy of post-structuralism and posthumanism, postmodernism dramatises the fact that everything that can be constructed and consumed can be treated as a text. This extends onto an understanding of such salient and seemingly abstract attributes such as memory, affect and embodiment as texts that can be endlessly deconstructed as well as reconstructed. In their ontological and formal complexities postmodernist poetics corroborate and dramatise one of the most quoted and contested sentences in critical theory, Jacques Derrida's "il n'y a pas de hors-texte" (*Limited Inc* 144), there is nothing outside of the text.

Works Cited

Adorno, Theodor. *Negative Dialectics*. Trans. E. B. Ashton. Frankfurt: Suhrkamp Verlag, 1966. Print.

Barth, John. "Night-Sea Journey." *Lost in the Funhouse*. London: Seeker & Warburg, 1969. Print.

Barthes, Roland. *Critical Essays*. Trans. Richard Howard. Evanston, IL: Northwestern UP, 1972. Print.

---. *Image Music Text*. Trans. Stephen Heath. New York: Hill & Wang, 1977. Print.

---. *Roland Barthes by Roland Barthes*. Trans. Richard Howard. Berkeley: U of California P, 1977. Print.

---. "To Write: An Intransitive Verb?" *The Structuralist Controversy: The Languages of Criticism and the Science of Man*. Ed. R. Macksey and E. Donato. Baltimore, MD: John Hopkins UP, 1972. 134–44. Print.

Baudrillard, Jean. *Simulations*. Trans. P. Foss, P. Patton and P. Beitchman. New York: Semiotext, 1983. Print.

Brecht, Bertolt. *Brecht on Theatre: The Development of an Aesthetic*. Ed. and Trans. John Willett. New York: Hill & Wang, 1964. Print.

Deleuze, Gilles. *Proust and Signs: The Complete Text*. Trans. Richard Howard. London: The Althone Press, 2000. Print.

Deleuze, Gilles, and Félix Guattari. *A Thousand Plateaus: Capitalism and Schizophrenia*. Trans. Brian Massumi. Minneapolis & London: U of Minnesota P, 1987. Print.

Derrida, Jacques. *Acts of Literature*. Ed. Derek Attridge. New York: Routledge, 1992. Print.

---. *De la grammatologie*. Paris: Minuit, 1967. Print.

---. *Limited Inc*. Evanston, IL: Northwestern UP, 1988. Print.

---. *Of Grammatology*. Trans. Gayatri Chakravorty Spivak. Baltimore, MD: John Hopkins UP, 1974. Print.

---. *Positions*. Trans. Alan Bass. Chicago, IL: U of Chicago P, 1981. Print.

---. "The Animal That Therefore I Am." *Critical Inquiry* 28.2 (Winter 2002): 369–418. Print.

---. "Two Words for Joyce." *Post-structuralist Joyce: Essays from the French*. Ed. Derek Attridge and Daniel Ferrer. Cambridge: Cambridge UP, 1984. 145–60. Print.

---. "Voice ii" (letter to Verena Andermatt Conley). *Boundary 2* 12.2 (1984): 76–93. Print.

---. *Writing and Difference*. Trans. Alan Bass. Chicago, IL: U of Chicago P, 1978. Print.

Foucault, Michel. *The Archaeology of Knowledge: And the Discourse on Language*. Trans. A. M. Sheridan Smith. New York: Pantheon, 1972. Print.

---. *The History of Sexuality: Volume I: An Introduction*. Trans. Robert Hurley. New York: Vintage, 1980. Print.

Fowles, John. *The French Lieutenant's Woman*. London: Triad/ Panther, 1976. Print.

---. *The Magus*. London: Jonathan Cape, 1966. Print.

Gay, Peter. *Style in History*. New York: Basic, 1974. Print.

Haraway, Donna. "A Cyborg Manifesto: Science, Technology and Socialist-Feminism in the Late Twentieth Century." *Simians, Cyborg and Women: The Reinvention of Nature*. New York: Routledge, 1991. 149–82. Print.

Hofstadter, Douglas. *Gödel, Escher, Bach: An Eternal Golden Braid*. Harmondsworth: Penguin Books, 1980. Print.

Hutcheon, Linda. *A Poetics of Postmodernism: History, Theory, Fiction*. London: Verso, 1984. Print.

---. *Narcissistic Narrative: The Metafictional Paradox*. Waterloo, Ontario: Wilfrid Laurier UP, 1980. Print.

Huyssen, Andreas. "Mapping the Postmodern." *New German Critique* (Autumn 1984): 5–52. Print.

Jameson, Fredric. "'In the Destructive Element Immerse': Hans-Jürgen Syberberg and Cultural Revolution." *October* 17 (Summer 1981): 99–118. Print.

---. *Postmodernism, or, the Cultural Logic of Late Capitalism*. Durham, NC: Duke UP, 1991. Print.

Katz, Steve. *The Exaggerations of Peter Prince*. New York: Holt, 1968. Print.

Krauss, Lawrence M. "Tangled up in Entanglement." *The New Yorker*. 31 Oct. 2015. Web. 29 June. 2018. <https://www.newyorker.com/tech/elements/tangled-up-in-entanglement-quantum-mechanics>.

Krauss, Rosalind. "Poststructuralism and the 'Paraliterary'." *October* 13 (Summer 1980): 36–40. Print.

Lyotard, Jean-François. *The Postmodern Condition: A Report on Knowledge*. Trans. Geoff Bennington and Brian Massumi. Manchester: Manchester UP, 1984. Print.

Major, Clarence. *Reflex and Bone Structure*. New York: Fiction Collective, 1975. Print.

McHale, Brian. *Postmodernist Fiction*. London: Methuen, 1987. Print.

Nietzsche, Friedrich. *The Use and Abuse of History*. Trans. Adrian Collins. New York: Liberal Arts Press, 1957. Print.

O'Brien, Flann. *At Swim-Two-Birds*. Hardmondsworth: Penguin Books, 1975. Print.

Pynchon, Thomas. *Bleeding Edge*. New York: Penguin Books, 2013. Print.

---. *Gravity's Rainbow*. New York: Viking, 1973. Print.

Ricardou, Jean. "Réalités variables, variantes réelles." *Problèmes du nouveau roman*. Paris: Seuil, 1967. 23–43. Print.

Sloterdijk, Peter. *Critique of Cynical Reason*. Trans. Michael Eldred. Minneapolis & London: U of Minnesota P, 1987. Print.

Thiher, Allen. *Words in Reflection: Modern Language Theory and Postmodern Fiction*. Chicago, IL: U of Chicago P, 1984. Print.

Waugh, Patricia. *Metafiction: Theory and Practice of Self-Conscious Fiction*. London & New York: Routledge, 1984. Print.

White, Hayden. "The Fictions of Factual Representations." *The Literature of Fact*. Ed. Angus Fletcher. New York: Columbia UP, 1976. 21–44. Print.

Notes

1. Ironic corroboration, along with a carnivalesque order of mimicry and fabulation, may be considered one of the premier postmodernist techniques of textual production.
2. It is interesting to observe that the term avant-garde quite literally means a state of situatedness that is always ahead, and is thus a natural description of the permanent prolepsis mentioned above. The postmodern avant-garde and its complex relationship with mainstream mass culture are examined by a number of theorists, including Peter Bürger, Renato Poggioli and Clement Greenberg.
3. The term Entanglement originates from Quantum Theory where it signifies a ceaseless generation of and interaction among particles whereby the quantum state of each particle may not be defined individually. For a funny and postmodernist

take on Entanglement in Quantum Physics, see "Tangled Up in Entanglement" by Lawrence M. Krauss (https://www.newyorker.com/tech/elements/tangled-up-in-entanglement-quantum-mechanics).

4. Derrida here offers a brilliant deconstructionist examination of Franz Kafka's "Before the Law" and how it subverts the expected economy of truth, fiction and justice with its endless entanglement of difference and deferring. The significance of Derrida and Deconstruction for postmodernist poetics will be studied in a subsequent section of this chapter and elsewhere in this book.
5. Patricia Waugh argues how the thriller is innately suited to be metafictional in narrative quality. Citing examples of postmodernist writers such as Thomas Pynchon, Italo Calvino, Anthony Burgess and Muriel Spark, Waugh examines how the thriller, with its "fear of anomie, of disorder, of the insecurity of human life" (84) lends itself to the metafictional self-reflexive poetics of postmodernist writing. Waugh goes on to examine how in Vladimir Nabokov's *Pale Fire*, the thriller form is experimentally explored and exploited to produce "the dizziness of a total loss of self" (84).
6. The term 'intertextuality' was largely popularised by the French feminist and critical theorist Julia Kristeva and refers to the referential nature of textual production whereby a text refers to, reflects and revisits earlier texts in a bid to revise as well as to retell. Intertextuality may be used as an interrogative method whereby the presuppositions of an earlier text are dramatised as well as deconstructed.
7. This endless alliance with other networks of knowledge that characterises postmodernist theory as well as fiction is perhaps best described by the structure of the rhizome, made famous in critical theory by the philosophers Gilles Deleuze and Félix Guattari. I will refer to the rhizome and to Deleuze and Guattari's works in more detail later in this chapter and also elsewhere.
8. It is interesting to note how the architectural legacy of postmodernism is referred to and revisited in Thomas Pynchon's 2013 novel *Bleeding Edge*, where a summer retreat is described

as a "postmodern" house with "circle and pieces of circle in the windows and framing" (191).

9. In this excellent work on language and postmodernist fabulation, Thiher examines how the foundations of narrative history were permanently unsettled by the works of Wittgenstein, Heidegger and Saussure, to be followed by the Deconstruction of Derrida.
10. A similar strategy features in Paul Auster's 2008 novel *Man in the Dark* which explores civil war and metafictionlised figures in a post–9/11 USA, narrated from the point of view of an ageing and decaying novelist.
11. Robert Young, in his remarkable work *White Mythologies: Writing History and the West* (1990) examines the Eurocentric epistemology of history writing and historical knowledge. One of the most notable claims Young makes at the very beginning of his book is to attribute the birth and growth of post-structuralism not so much to the student riots in Paris but to the development of the Algerian War of independence.
12. In her influential work on metafiction, Patricia Waugh makes an interesting analogy between the metafictional aesthetics of postmodernist poetics and Heisenberg's Uncertainty Principle. Waugh, however, problematises it further by stating that while the Heisenbergian uncertainty at least allows a partial or relational description of nature apropos of the situatedness of the subject, metafiction explores the dilemma of describing from being situated within a prisonhouse of language (4). Waugh's distinction seems to support and corroborate the ontological distinction between uncertainty and certaintylessness as described in this chapter.
13. The stylistic, artistic and discursive differences between the Joyce of *Ulysses* and the Joyce of *Finnegans Wake* bear testimony to the attitudinal difference between modernism and postmodernism.
14. The term carnivalesque as used here and later in this book largely draws on the work of Mikhail Bakhtin (1895–1975) whose retelling of Rabelais forms one of the foundational moments in postmodernist critical theory. Bakhtin is also credited with introducing terms such as polyphony, heteroglossia and

chronotope (a complex of space time) that bears remarkable resonance with the Einsteinian notion of the relative universe with a fluid sense of space and time. I will refer to and draw on Bakhtin more extensively in the subsequent chapters of this book.

15. Evidently anticipating the later works of Slavoj Žižek, Sloterdijk situates the situational against the claims of the universal and decodes the latter – in political and philosophical discourses as well as in war – as a network of strategies that are best studied with cynicism. The spirit of cynicism as theorised by Sloterdijk is one of the most compelling theses in postmodernist philosophy.
16. Examining the difference between Van Gogh's and Andy Warhol's paintings of shoes as examples of high-modernist and postmodernist forms of representation, Jameson reads those respectively as artistic products with ontological depth carrying the possibility of critique and as artifacts with ontological flatness and superficiality which Jameson describes as "perhaps the supreme formal feature of all the postmodernisms" (*Postmodernism* 10) that he studies subsequently.
17. Derrida's examination of the playful and subversive animality which extends onto a critique of the Cartesian cognitive essence clearly anticipates current works on Animal Studies and posthumanism which have their very foundation in an interrogation of the binaries between the human and the non-human, the organic and the inorganic.
18. In Haraway's analysis, bourgeois realism inhabits the same discursive plane as that of biological determinism, scientific management and white capitalist patriarchy, some of the very foundational principles extending from the spirit of European Enlightenment against which postmodernism situates itself.

ONE

Memory, History and Identities in Postmodern Narratives

In Thomas Pynchon's 2013 novel *Bleeding Edge*, Reg Despard, who makes a living in the 1990s by selling cheap, pirated semi-pornographic film cassettes in New York streets even as he struggles to steady his camcorder inside noisy cinema halls, happens to accidentally discover the zoom feature in his handheld device. He then proceeds to playfully capture details of human anatomy, extras in crowd and offbeat fast-moving cars behind the protagonists on screen. Immediately afterwards, on a seemingly uneventful day, Reg Despard sells a pirated movie-cassette to a film studies professor at NYU who rushes back to him the very next morning to inform him that his work is way ahead of the most cutting-edge filming techniques of post–postmodern cinematography, going on to describe Reg's recording style as the "neo-Brechtian subversion of the diegesis" (9). Subsequently, Reg finds himself frequently invited to deliver demonstrations to doctoral students of film studies and gains enough money and fame to shoot his own films.

Pynchon's novel, which is about the collapse of the dot-com boom and the exhaustion of IT capital in post–9/11 USA, presents one of the finest features of postmodernist poetics, the fast and seemingly random mutability of meaning and identity, whereby the borderlines between scholarship and showmanship, culture and kitsch, are perilously slippery. Reg's abrupt elevation from a seller of bootlegged movie videos to an experimental film-maker is less due to a deliberate decision or prodigious performance than due to an order of randomness and reception that incorporates fate, quirkiness and coincidence. At once ridiculous and eventful, self-conscious and self-effacing, fateful and funny, postmodernist poetics frequently dramatises a circus of identities that are plastic and performative. This is most evident in novels that juxtapose private narratives alongside historical narratives, drawing on the picaresque tradition of storytelling and presenting quasi-clowns as protagonists who painfully and accidentally become benchmarks of history and historical knowledge. One of the finest examples of this in postmodernist fiction is Salman Rushdie's *Midnight's Children* (1981).

A magnificent performance in postmodernist poetics, Rushdie's novel may indeed be considered as an entanglement of history and fiction, magic and reality, with its unreliable narration, erroneous accounts of events and incidents and self-reflexive storytelling that often becomes metafictional in its scope. With a clown–magician as a protagonist "mysteriously handcuffed to history" (3), having been born at the stroke of midnight when India became independent, *Midnight's Children* is marked by the deliberate excesses and eccentricities that characterise postmodernist fiction. It appropriates a recognisable mythic method of storytelling – that of the Scheherazade in *One Thousand and One Nights* – and bastardises it relentlessly by juxtaposing real historical events and figures with fictional phenomena and metafictional episodes. With its carnivalesque quality, heteroglossic imagination and metonymic allegory of the national narrative, Rushdie's *Midnight's Children* is also a premier example of postcolonial writing. The novel becomes an example of subversion through mimicry, positioning the "performative present" (Bhabha 35) – against any ontology of origin.

The fragmented, disintegrated and interstitial quality of the chronicler of the nation is elaborately described in Rushdie's novel, while also approximating the metafictional mode acutely aware of its own constructed cosmos:

> Please believe that I am falling apart.
>
> I am not speaking metaphorically; nor is this the opening gambit of some melodramatic, riddling, grubby appeal for pity. I mean quite simply that I have begun to crack all over like an old jug – that my poor body, singular, unlovely, buffeted by too much history, subjected to drainage above and drainage below, mutilated by doors, brained by spittoons, has started coming apart at the seams. In short, I am literally disintegrating, slowly for the moment, although there are signs of acceleration. I ask you only to accept (as I have accepted) that I shall eventually crumble into (approximately) six hundred and thirty million particles of anonymous, and necessarily oblivious dust. This is why I have resolved to confide in paper, before I forget. (We are a nation of forgetters.) (43)

If the body of Saleem Sinai bears an indexical correspondence to the new nation consumed and hunted by history, its disintegration is reflective of the pulls and polyphony of voices that the hegemonic national narrative cannot contain. The description of the decadent body apropos of historical agency in Rushdie's novel bears interesting resonance with Michel Foucault's description of the self: "totally imprinted by history and the process of history's destruction of the body" (148). Excessive as well as minimalistic, unreal as well as unreliable, bombastic as well as bathetic, Saleem Sinai in *Midnight's Children*, like Oskar Matzerath – the magical dwarf-drummer in Günter Grass's *The Tin Drum* – embodies as well as enacts a *tour de force* in postmodernist storytelling. With an olfactory sensibility far above the average level and a story that smacks of leaked history, Saleem Sinai in Rushdie's novel embodies the entanglement of the super-sensory body and the super-sized nation, inhabiting "those hairlines along which history and sexuality moved" (Rushdie 125).

As a mutable mosaic of India's post–imperial nation-formation, *Midnight's Children* is a brilliant bricolage of memories, stories and identities that operate across an overarching historical narrative, informing as well as problematising the latter in its enunciative process. Rushdie's *writerly* text is less a seamless saga of a new nation than a notoriously slippery story that incorporates the magical and the mundane orders in an endless tragicomic *telos*. "Cutting up history" to "suit" his "nefarious purposes" (360), Saleem Sinai in Rushdie's *Midnight's Children* enacts the *trompe l'oeil* techniques typical of postmodernist fiction whereby an embedded unreal world is superimposed over the real narrative landscape. This is done by deliberately foregrounding the production of constraints and by manipulative narration (Hutcheon 81), playing tricks on the reader and other characters alike. In true postmodernist style, what Saleem Sinai offers is less a stable story than a series of "[i]nterruptions, nothing but interruptions", slippages with a "wholly unreasonable obstinacy, to stay neatly in their separate compartments" (259).

The entanglement of interruptions and unreliable stories corresponds to what Saleem in *Midnight's Children* famously refers to as the "chutnification of history; the grand hope of the pickling of time" (642). It also dramatises an order of knowledge which "shortens its vision to those things nearest to it – the body, the nervous system, nutrition, digestion, and energies" (Foucault 155). This produces not only a carnivalesque quality that calls into question grand narratives of national figures and phenomena but also a mimicry of the model of the nation itself. A literal embodiment of imagined communities,[1] the conference of magical midnight's children in Rushdie's novel emerges as a surreal *séance* of supernatural figures that undercuts the constructed rationale and mapped demography of nation-formation. Instead of the seamless certainty of national knowledge, *Midnight's Children* offers fractures and fault lines focalised through a magical clown-chronicler whose accidental identity is informed largely by what *does not happen*.

Midnight's Children presents a protagonist who blurs the borderlines between illusion and reality, not as a nostalgic voice lamenting the loss of origins but as the main mouthpiece of a carnivalesque chorus that celebrates centrelessness. This is made amply evident in many sections of the novel, not least in Saleem's description of the relativity of reality in the chapter entitled "All-India Radio":

> Reality is a question of perspective; the further you get from the past, the more concrete and plausible it seems – but as you approach the present, it inevitably seems more and more incredible. Suppose yourself in a large cinema, sitting at first in the back row, and gradually moving up, row by row, until your nose is almost pressed against the screen. Gradually the stars' faces dissolve into dancing grain; tiny details assume grotesque proportions; the illusion dissolves – or rather, it becomes clear that the illusion itself is reality. (229)

The perspectival quality of reality and, by extension, of history itself, is dramatised in keeping with the claims of postmodern historians such as Hayden White, that what appears true or real in historiography "wears the mask of a meaning, the completeness and fullness of which we can only imagine, never experience" ("The Value of Narrativity" 24). Imagination and fabulation, instead of objectivisation and knowledge-preservation, inform the postmodernist fiction that seeks to situate itself as what Jacques Derrida defined as "deconstructable history" (4) where "narrative positioning" becomes the tool for resisting the hegemony of "discursive inscription" (Hutcheon 97). As in E. L. Doctorow's *Ragtime* (1975) where real historical figures such as Harry Houdini, Sigmund Freud,[2] Henry Ford and Carl Jung appear as fictional characters and history appears in the end as "no more than a tune on a player piano" (Doctorow 270), *Midnight's Children* presents a collage of historical events and figures with fictional fantasies where the borderlines between what really happened and what could have happened are always unclear. The historical figures that appear in *Midnight's Children* include Indira Gandhi, Sanjay Gandhi, Ayub Khan and Zulfikar Ali Bhutto. What Rushdie's novel highlights is the dramatic and discursive quality informing history writing and how the same is concealed in standardised and shared accounts of events.

The textuality of history writing and the politics of language thereof are also dramatised in Rushdie's *Shame* (1983), which emerges as a metafictional allegory of the formation of Pakistan as a nation. The writing of Pakistani history was conducted in Urdu and English – both imported tongues – and the narrator confesses he had to "for ever alter what is written" (31). The "writing-shiting" (24) that Saleem Sinai performs in *Midnight's Children*, much to the exasperation and consternation of his immediate audience Padma who pesters him to have his meal instead, is a hopelessly and deliriously messy magic-realist act that extends the limits of historical knowledge even as it destroys the "unities and conventions of fine writing" (328).

As in Robert Coover's *The Public Burning* (1977) where Richard Nixon attempts to seduce Ethel Rosenberg at Sing Sing Prison on the night of her execution and Stanley Elkin's *The Living End* (1979) where the tennis superstar Ilie Năstase is overheard by the dead yet still conscious Ladlehaus from the latter's grave close to a tennis court, history in *Midnight's Children* is essentially a play between facticity and fantasy. This is appropriately articulated by the narrator who is "prepared to distort everything – to re-write the whole history" of his times, solely in order to place himself "in a central role" (230). In true postmodernist spirit, the unreliability of Saleem Sinai as a narrator and chronicler of history is highlighted by Rushdie himself in a now-famous essay entitled "'Errata': or, Unreliable Narration in *Midnight's Children*" where he underlines the epistemological and discursive difference between Rushdie the writer and Saleem the narrator. Acknowledging his own research errors in the novel – most significantly his erroneous description of General Dyer's troops during the Amritsar Massacre on 13 April 1919 – while also stating his reluctance to rectify those in subsequent editions, Rushdie describes how the "wrongness feels *right*" ("Errata" 23, italics in original) in the mutable map of Saleem's unreliable narration. In doing so, he articulates the ambivalence and plurality that inform postmodernist poetics, whereby epistemological errors are "tipped over" becoming ontological questions (McHale 11). The key issue here is the politics of representation whereby historical events such as the Amritsar Massacre and Auschwitz are sometimes deliberately defamiliarised and thus dramatise what Toni Morrison in *Beloved* (1987) describes as *rememory*, the aporetic after-image that lies outside shared cultural narratives and resists any classification into coherent meanings.

Beloved, one of the finest achievements in twentieth–century American literature, is a novel about slavery, spectrality and traumatic repetition. But underlying its fictional topography is the drama of memory or traumatic memory that presents not so much a story as the story's situatedness at an embodied level outside of the shared cultural narrative. In true postmodernist fashion, *Beloved* opens up the binary between reality and spectrality, between materiality and memory, with the trope of rememory emerging as an intersubjective economy of imagined pasts. Morrison's novel unfolds as a play between matter and its absence where "[s]ifting daylight dissolves the memory, turns it into dust motes floating in light" (Morrison 309). The postmodernist plasticity of space, time and the changing mind is dramatised in *Beloved* in the way in which rememory emerges as an act of reconstruction that may not be real but may still be shared at subjective as well as intersubjective levels. This is described thus:

> Some things go. Pass on. Some things just stay. I used to think it was my rememory. . . . But it's not. Places, places are still there.

> If a house burns down, it's gone, but the place—the picture of it—stays, and not just in my rememory, but out there, in the world. . . . Someday you be walking down the road and you hear something or see something going on. So clear. And you think it's you thinking it up. A thought picture. But no. It's when you bump into a rememory that belongs to somebody else. (40–41)

Beloved dramatises the affective after-image (Moglen 35) in memory that informs as well as interrogates history and the production of historical knowledge. In turning a personal and quasi-supernatural story into an allegory of slavery and its traumatic repetitions, Morrison appropriates a postmodernist poststructuralist narrative method that undercuts the rationale of bourgeois classic realism with an entanglement of the Gothic and the fantastic. In true postmodernist spirit, *Beloved* "nudges at the edges of definitions – of conscious and unconscious impulses and motivations, of life and death, of the real and the fantasised" (Lucas 46).

Rushdie's highlighting of the deliberate unreliability and historical inaccuracy embedded in *Midnight's Children* points to an important issue that interests researchers in memory studies today, the distinction between *literal truth* and *remembered truth*, and the proclivity of the human mind to prioritise the latter in the imaginary landscape that storytelling inhabits. The postmodernist poetics of unreliable narration and unreal recall correspond closely to recent research in cognitive psychology about the essentially incomplete quality of human memory. Rushdie's description of his own memory of the 1962 India–China War is particularly telling in this context:

> . . . one of the simplest truths about any set of memories is that many of them will be false. I myself have a clear memory of having been in India during the China War. I 'remember' how frightened we all were, I 'recall' people making nervy little jokes about needing to buy themselves a Chinese phrase book or two, because the Chinese Army was not expected to stop until it reached Delhi.

> I also know that I could not possibly have been in India at that time. I was interested to find that *even after I found out that my memory was playing tricks* my brain simply refused to unscramble itself. It clung to the false memory, preferring it to mere literal happenstance. I thought that was an important lesson to learn. ("Errata" 24, italics in original)

Rushdie's description of the unreliability of memory and the plasticity of the remembering mind more prone to creative insertions than accurate preservations, finds remarkable resonance in recent research by neuroscientists such as the Nobel Laureate Eric Kandel, who in his book on memory states unequivocally that "[w]hen people try to recollect a story, for example, they sometimes make creative errors, deleting some parts of the story, fabricating other parts, and generally trying to reconstruct the information in a way that makes sense" (85). The neuroscientific corroboration of the imaginative quality of memory and the reconstructive quality of the remembering process finds its extreme example in the postmodernist proclivity towards multidimensional memory, perhaps most famously instantiated in Carlos Fuentes's *Terranostra* (1975) that offers a fictional history of Spanish America. In keeping with the intertextuality informing postmodernist poetics, Fuentes's novel features Cervantes sentenced to death for writing Kakfa's *Metamorphosis* prematurely, thus bringing into play not just a mosaic of historical events but also an entanglement of real writers and fictional works as characters and consequences in true postmodernist fashion. This complex of fictionality and intertextuality is common in postmodernist poetics as seen in Gilbert Sorrentino's *Imaginative Qualities of Actual Things* (1971) where a character's wife is named Lolita with the narrator emphasising in an immediate and heavy-handed way that she is the same Lolita of fiction: "the exact Lolita that Nabokov stitched together" (193). The role of memory in Fuentes's novel is particularly poignant. In the episodes from a Theatre of Memory, where known and factually recognised historical events are deliberately distorted, the reader sees Calpurnia holding back Caesar from attending the Senate on the Ides of March, Socrates refusing the poison that would kill him, a baby girl instead of a boy born in a stable during the reign of Augustus and Columbus on a camel visiting the court of Genghis Khan.

The buffet of creative anachronisms and imaginative insertions in Fuentes's novel is followed with a telling description of alternate possibilities that emerge as the true business of postmodernist historiographic metafiction: "[h]istory repeats itself only because we are unaware of the alternate possibility for each historic event: what that event could have been but was not. Knowing, we can insure that history does not repeat itself; that the alternate possibility is the one that occurs for the first time" (644). Like other postmodernist writers such as William S. Burroughs, Fuentes deploys the motif of time travel in order to underline the entanglement of private memory and historical situatedness in his novel. Thus, in *Terranostra*, a twentieth-century Parisian traveller goes back in time to Spain's *Siglo de Oro* (Golden Age) as the novel itself emerges as a counter-history that celebrates its inaccuracies and incongruities. In postmodernist fiction, historical time is also sliced up in terms of attributes as fictional figures are characterised anachronistically, as in John Fowles's *The French Lieutenant's Woman* (1969) where the heroine Sarah Woodruff, despite being a mid-nineteenth-century woman, is dressed in attributes typical of a mid-twentieth-century person. Such creative anachronisms abound in Fowles's novel which describes a Victorian home in terms of the absence of television and maps a nineteenth-century Lyme landscape with an aerial view.

The metafictionality in Fowles's novel is entangled with the inaccuracies and deliberate distortions of history and historical identity while also alluding directly to key currents in critical theory. The result is, as in Rushdie's *Midnight's Children*, a complex of frustration and fantasy that dramatises the discourse of storytelling itself:

> I do not know. This story I am telling is all imagination. These characters I create never existed outside my own mind. If I have pretended until now to know my characters' minds and innermost thoughts, it is because I am writing in (just as I have assumed some of the vocabulary and 'voice' of) a convention universally accepted at the time of my story: that the novelist stands next to God. He may not know all, yet he tries to pretend that he does. But I live in the age of Alain Robbe-Grillet and Roland Barthes; if this is a novel, it cannot be a novel in the modern sense of the word.
>
> So perhaps I am writing a transposed autobiography; perhaps I now live in one of the houses I have brought into the fiction; perhaps Charles is myself disguised. Perhaps it is only a game. Modern women like Sarah exist, and I have never understood them. Or perhaps I am trying to pass off a concealed book of essays on you. Instead of chapter headings, perhaps I should have written 'On the Horizontality of Existence,' 'The Illusions of Progress,' 'The History of the Novel Form,' 'The Aetiology of Freedom,' 'Some Forgotten Aspects of the Victorian Age'... what you will. (95)

The passage above mixes history with literary traditions, materiality with imagination, in a way that is typical of postmodernist poetics. The digressive, subversive quality of the content is further underlined in Fowles's flashing of the chapter number, 13, and by the additional attack against "the capitalized ghosts" (98) of Time, Progress, Society and Evolution.

In deconstructing and questioning its very own authorial codes, Fowles's narrator here delineates the distinction between classic–realist omniscient narration and the postmodernist unreliable narration, associating the latter with contemporary currents in critical thought. The reference to Roland Barthes, of course, underlines the death of the author but Fowles extends it further by dramatising the dilemma between storytelling and autobiography, a theme that immediately highlights the postmodernist play between history and fantasy. *The French Lieutenant's Woman* foregrounds freshness and incongruity – juxtaposing the aristocratic paleontologist Charles Smithson with the Victorian *femme fatale* Sarah Woodruff – and dramatises how the same can be a strategy to rewrite and revise history from "always this being caught in the same fiendish machine" (207).

The allusion to Barthes in *The French Lieutenant's Woman* is significant also in the context of Barthes's own playful autobiography which emerges as an entanglement of fact and fiction, as examined in the introduction of this book. What is questioned in the passage above, and in several instances in Fowles's novel, is the epistemological process informing the process of writing itself. The ontological divide between autobiography and the act of writing the same, and the postmodernist proclivity to blur this very divide is powerfully described by the Deconstructionist Paul de Man thus:

> We assume that life *produces* the autobiography as an act produces its consequences, but can we not suggest, with equal justice, that the autobiographical project may itself produce and determine the life and that whatever the writer *does* is in fact governed by the technical demands of self-portraiture and thus determined in all its aspects by the resources of his medium. (920, italics in original)

In other words, rather than reading the autobiography as the neat narrative of what happened in *real life*, postmodernist poetics inverts the order and reads the lived life as the narrative that follows the written word. This is in keeping with Barthes's autobiography that deliberately draws on a fictional narrative structure and declares itself a novel. But de Man's description also corresponds to the broader project of Deconstruction itself, one articulated by Derrida in *Of Grammatology*, about subverting the Eurocentric phallogocentric supremacy of the sign. Instead of viewing the written word as a simple delineation of the speech act, as defined by Enlightenment thinkers such as Rousseau, Derrida describes writing as an act that "threatened the desire for the living speech from the closest proximity, it *breached* living speech from within and from the very beginning" (56–57, italics in original). Postmodernist poetics often emerges as a celebration of such breach, whereby the desired continuity of the living speech and, by extension, of the shared narrative, is endlessly interrupted. In the process it plays up historical identities and the ontology of historical knowledge itself.

Fowles's *The French Lieutenant's Woman* is a benchmark in postmodernist poetics due to its production of fictional identities that subvert historical objectivity as well as authorial intentionality. Far from being a flashy phenomenon, the allusion to Barthes is an admission of postmodernist creativity that relies less on authorial control than on unreliable and facetious fallouts:

> *we wish to create worlds as real as, but other than the world that is*. Or was. This is why we cannot plan. We know a world is an organism, not a machine. We also know that a genuinely created world must be independent of its creator; a planned world (a world that fully reveals its planning) is a dead world. It is only when our characters and events begin to disobey us that they begin to live. When Charles left Sarah on her cliff-edge, I ordered him to walk straight back to Lyme Regis. But he did not; he gratuitously turned and went down to the Dairy. (96, italics in original)

The notion of the world as a living organism as opposed to a passively functioning machine is testimony to the postmodernist acceptance of messiness and mutability instead of classification and facticity. The organicity of the postmodernist character lies precisely in its disobedience that undercuts any ontology of authorial control and completion. The freedom of Fowles's fictional characters is not absolute or constant – thus resisting any form of closure – but they are free to be reconstructed in a creatively receptive reader's imagination and reintegrated into other scripts or forms of media such as cinema (Waugh 125).

What is dramatised in *The French Lieutenant's Woman* is not an absolute death of the author but a location in a third space – that of the mimetic map, in its remappings and revisions. It is similar to the "I" in Jorge Luis Borges's "Borges and I" in *Labyrinths* (1962), who explicitly articulates his autonomy as well as entanglement in relation to his creator–writer thus:

> I live, let myself go on living, so that Borges may contrive his literature, and this literature justifies me. It is no effort for me to confess that he has achieved some valid pages, but those pages cannot save me, perhaps because what is good belongs to no one, not even to him, but rather to the language and to tradition. (282)

This carnivalesque quality spills over onto the domain of events as well and informs the postmodernist problematisation of objective and universal truth, a project that may be traced back to Nietzsche as examined in the introduction. Fowles's narrator in *The French Lieutenant's Woman* is, however, also aware of the impossibility of perfect centrelessness and admits that even the most avant-garde postmodernist writing cannot entirely extirpate the presence of the author. He is quick to add though – and this is the crucial ontological shift – that the nature of the presence has altered. In other words, "what has changed is that we are no longer the gods of the Victorian image, omniscient and decreeing; but in the new theological image, with freedom our first principle, not authority" (97). This spirit is in perfect correspondence with the postmodernist proclivity to examine historical events, like religions and social positions, as "opium fantasies" (207). *The French Lieutenant's Woman* plays with shared notions of time, space and storytelling. In the process it generates a plethora of identities that are complexes of historical as well as fictional truth, drawing on a mutable map of historical as well as fictional memory typical of postmodernist writing.

Fowles achieves the right blend of history and historiography in *The French Lieutenant's Woman* through his characterisation of the figure of Sarah Woodruff, who is described in the introduction as "a figure from myth, than any proper fragment of the petty provincial day" (9). His relationship with his character Sarah – who may be described as a postmodern muse – is comparable to that of Clarence Major's relationship with the character Cora Hull in *Reflex and Bone Structure* (1975). In the latter novel, Cora Hull seduces her author with the words attributed to her that linger on her like bodies and clothes. This is in keeping with the famous pronouncement made by Borges who drew on Carlyle while stating that "the history of the universe is an infinite sacred book that all men write and read and try to understand, and in which they are also written" (*Labyrinths* 231). Within such narrative politics, life and fiction share an intertextual intersubjective relationship whereby private memory and shared history are endlessly intertwined. Everything becomes a text that can be deconstructed and reconstructed. The Derridean philosophy is thus vindicated. There is no outside of the text.

The entanglement of memory, history, storytelling and identity in postmodernist fiction is also powerfully exemplified in the works of Italo Calvino, whose *Invisible Cities* (1972) is notionally set in thirteenth-century China visited by Marco Polo and marked by the relentless invasions of the Tartar empire. Calvino is, of course, one of the finest practitioners of postmodernist metafiction as exemplified by the inimitable *If on a Winter's Night a Traveller* (1979), which explicitly addresses the reader in second person and foregrounds the "supremacy of his or her activity in realizing the text imaginatively" (Waugh 43) while dramatically drawing attention to the fictional and constructed quality of the text itself:

> You are about to begin reading Italo Calvino's new novel, *If on a winter's night a traveler.* Relax. Concentrate. Dispel every other thought. Let the world around you fade. Best to close the door; the TV is always on in the next room. Tell the others right away, 'No, I don't want to watch TV!' Raise your voice – they won't hear you otherwise – 'I'm reading! I don't want to be disturbed!' Maybe they haven't heard you, with all that racket; speak louder, yell: 'I'm beginning to read Italo Calvino's new novel!' Or if you prefer, don't say anything; just hope they'll leave you alone. (Calvino 3)

In *The Castle of Crossed Destinies* (1969), Calvino dramatises the generative and combinational quality of narrative and narrative production by showcasing a group of mute men producing tales by picking and combining images from a pack of tarot cards while the stories thus generated emerge in varied differential qualities in relation to certain archetypal narratives: *Oedipus Rex*, *The Grail Legend*, *King Lear*, *Hamlet* and *Macbeth*. This automatised mode of self-reflexive storytelling through combination achieves its highest point in Calvino in *If on a Winter's Night,* which pushes its metafictionality to its extreme by describing the reader in the act of reading the same novel which "begins in a railway station . . . a cloud of smoke hides part of the first paragraph" (10). The constructed quality of the novel is constantly highlighted and dramatised by the authorial attention foregrounding missing pages, pages stuck together and deliberately disordered pagination. It is a narrative that explicitly states that "memory is true as long as you do not set it, as long as it is not enclosed in a form" (181). Through its metafictional architectonic, *If on a Winter's Night a Traveller* arguably achieves the finest form of formlessness and fictionality that characterises postmodernist poetics.

While *If on a Winter's Night a Traveller* produces metafictional and intertextual identities, Calvino's *Invisible Cities* (1972) produces a postmodernist kaleidoscope of historical and fantastical identities that inhabit real as well as magic realist landscapes. Among the unreal spaces that feature in *Invisible Cities* are Penthesilea, characterised by endless and centreless suburbs, Cecilia, a city that increasingly incorporates all surrounding spaces, and Trude, a city that "does not begin and does not end. Only the name of the airport changes" (128). This is in keeping with Michel Foucault's description of heterotopias as spaces that "secretly undermine language, because they make it impossible to name this and that, and because they destroy 'syntax' in advance . . . that apparent syntax which causes words and things (next to and also opposite to one another) to 'hold together'" (*The Order of Things* xviii). In true postmodernist fashion, *Invisible Cities* foregrounds a play of memory, history and spatiality that constantly constructs and reconstructs identities. It dramatises the impossibility of absolute knowledge and showcases instead how the desire for emblems ends up becoming an emblem in itself, in an infinite sea of signifiers with no complete closure. This is evinced in the exchange between the traveller Marco Polo and the emperor Kublai Khan:

> *The new fact received a meaning from that emblem and also added to the emblem a new meaning. Perhaps, Kublai thought, the empire is nothing but a zodiac of the mind's phantasms.*
>
> *'On the day when I know all the emblems,' he asked Marco, 'shall I be able to possess my empire, at last?'*
>
> *And the Venetian answered: 'Sire, do not believe it. On that day you will be an emblem among emblems'.* (22–23, italics in original)

Among other things, Calvino's *Invisible Cities* highlights the flickering and shadowy quality of space and time, one that questions the constancy of signs and the hubris of historical knowledge alike.

Along with a complex play of spaces and signifiers, much of postmodernist fiction engages with innovative orders and representations of time and remembrance of times past. Thus, Martin Amis's *Time's Arrow* (1991) tells a Holocaust narrative backwards, where time "pours past unpreventably" and where Canada "is where young men hang out when they really ought to be in Vietnam" (58). Amis problematises his novel further by constantly questioning the ontology of memory and the remembering mind, thus dramatising the unreliability essentially embedded in postmodernist poetics. This is made amply evident in *Time's Arrow*:

> What is it with them, the human beings? I suppose they remember what they want to remember. And I suppose, in our case, John and I should exchange high fives in squalid thanks to this human talent for forgetting: forgetting, not as a process of erosion and waste, but as an activity. John forgets. Nurse Davis forgets. The husband, Dennis, shuddering in the cold on his way to work, on his way to watch the night, forgets. (80)

Amis's description of the entanglement of remembering and forgetting corresponds, like Rushdie's description of a nation of forgetters in *Midnight's Children*, to the neuroscientific notion of forgetting as an ability and activity that informs remembering, rather than being its organic obverse. It bears remarkable resemblance to Gabriel García Márquez's notions that memory rarely fails – despite old age – "with regard to things that are of real interest to us" (*Memories of My Melancholy Whores* 8) and that solitude can make a selection in memory, doing away with the "dimming piles of nostalgic waste" (*One Hundred Years of Solitude* 219) and purifying and magnifying the bitter ones. This notion of plastic memory and the identities generated therewith underlines the process that characterises the postmodernist play between the signifier and the signified, the actor and the event, the rememberer and the remembered. The result is a fictional manifestation of what critical theorists such as Catherine Malabou describe as the ambivalent osmosis of *plastic* and *graphic* forms of representation, whereby opposition and functionality take place simultaneously (3). Defining plasticity as the "*spontaneous organization of fragments*" (7, italics in original) that characterises the nervous system as well as representational techniques in writing, Malabou offers an excellent example of what might be considered a template for postmodernist fiction and historiography alike.

The theme of personal/autobiographical memory running against the narrative of objective history and the multidimensionality and unreliability embedded in the process is dramatised also in *Ada, or Ardor: A Family Chronicle* (1969) by Vladimir Nabokov, one of the most representative writers in the postmodernist tradition and perhaps the finest practitioner of unreliable narration in fiction. As in Roland Barthes's *Roland Barthes*, Nabokov's *Ada* foregrounds the fictionality embedded in any representation of memory. Incorporating issues such as joint narration, fantasy projection and metonymic memory, *Ada* also weaves in the stylistic features of science fiction and *roman à clef* while problematising both genres in the process. Its contesting perspectives come from the narrator–characters Van and Ada, while the anti-world of Antiterra is an entanglement of superimposed spaces and discontinuous chronology. Nabokov's novel also raises issues of nation, situatedness and memory, with real places such as Russia, France and USA superimposed on Estotiland, which emerges as a condensed *chronotope*[3] where memories of the peak periods in Nabokov's life – the innocence of his pre-Russian Revolution childhood, his early youth in the 1920s and his authorial success in the subsequent years – occupy a palpable present.

E. L. Doctorow's *Ragtime* (1975) carries the refrain, "[t]his was the time in our history" in its juxtaposition of historical and personal/fictional narratives. Thus, historical figures such as Winslow Homer, Jacob Riis and Theodore Dreiser appear and disappear in the novel as pointers to historical time against which the fictional cosmos unfolds itself. The fragmented quality of history and historical truth apropos of the fictionality and fantasy of memory manifests itself recurrently in postmodernist writing. It receives a remarkable depiction in Milan Kundera's *The Book of Laughter and Forgetting* (1979) where the Communist leader Clementis – subsequently assassinated by the Party and erased from public discourse – is only preserved in collective memory through the photo of his fur hat which he kindly took off from his own head and placed on the head of his fellow Communist Gottwald, right before the latter's lecture on a snowy day in 1948 Prague (3). Kundera's novel, which situates the agency of memory as a human resistance against power and the demand to forget, fictionalises the emplotment, unreliability and plasticity underlining the ontology of remembering and the production and preservation of historical identities. The metonymic memory of Clementis – "[n]othing remains of Clementis but the fur hat on Gottwald's head" (3–4) – is a pointer to the plasticity that characterises remembering and forgetting alike, at private as well as shared levels.

Like Rushdie's unreliable memory of the 1962 India–China War, Kundera's *The Book of Laughter and Forgetting* presents a case of fictionalised memory in a section entitled "Mama", where the eponymous character remembers herself as a young girl on stage in 1918 in the newly formed Republic of Czechoslovakia reciting a poem that celebrates the birth of the new republic and the demise of the Austrian Empire. Mama also remembers how she had forgotten the final stanza of the patriotic poem, how she had to make it up on stage and how the audience could not tell the difference while she herself had to subsequently rush to the bathroom in shame. However, as Mama's son Karel discloses immediately, Mama could not possibly have been a young schoolgirl during that time as she had already graduated by the time the war for freedom from the empire ended. More significantly, the poem that Mama mentions is part of a Christmas programme and not a patriotic piece at all.

However, Kundera seems to suggest, as does Rushdie in *Midnight's Children* and elsewhere, that the trick memory plays here, often with the knowledge of the rememberer herself, becomes an important constituent in the self-construction process that relies less on verification than on creative representation, emerging often at once as preservation and production through storytelling. Kundera's novel goes on to depict how Mama's son Karel allows himself to make creative recollections about his amorous adventures, claiming to have seen his friend's mother Nora naked in a spa. This piece of fabricated memory, along with his mother's opinion that Nora looks strikingly similar to Karel's friend Eva, makes Eva fantastically attractive in Karel's creative and manipulative memory. *The Book of Laughter and Forgetting* describes how Karel likens himself to a chess player while making love to his wife Marketa and his friend Eva: "he felt like a great chess player who has conquered opponents simultaneously on two chessboards . . . he couldn't help laughing and shouting, 'I'm Bobby Fischer! I'm Bobby Fischer!'" (67).

In true postmodernist fashion, the opening of *The Book of Laughter and Forgetting*, entitled "Lost Letters", describes a metafictional drama where the narrator explains how a character insists on inhabiting the opening space of his narrative, much to the consternation of the implied author, Mirek:

> His connection to his life was that of a sculptor to his statue or a novelist to his novel. It is an inviolable right of a novelist to rework his novel. If the opening does not please him, he can rewrite it or delete it. But Zdena's existence denied Mirek that author's prerogative. Zdena insisted on remaining on the opening pages of the novel and did not let herself be crossed out. (15)

What is immediately dramatised is the postmodernist proclivity towards storytelling agency and narrative emplotment in place of objective autobiography or history. As in Fowles's *The French Lieutenant's Woman*, the problematic proximity between real life and fictional narrative is evident but what complicates things even further is the element of narrative construction that Kundera's book highlights, one that underlines the ontological plasticity in the process of history-writing. This plasticity, although operative endlessly – as in the systematic effort of the Communist Party in Czechoslovakia to erase the memory of the figure of Clementis – is also effaced from the smooth seamlessness of hegemonic history.

As in Rushdie's *Midnight's Children* and Amis's *Time's Arrow*, Kundera in *Testaments Betrayed* (1993) states unequivocally that "[t]he present moment is unlike the memory of it. Remembering is not the negative of forgetting. Remembering is a form of forgetting" (128). This is in keeping with the postmodernist problematic between the signifier and the signified, whereby a sign and its opposite do not necessarily negate each other. What postmodernist works such as *Midnight's Children*, *Time's Arrow* and *Maus* (1986) dramatise is the narrative and constructed quality of memory-writing and history-writing. Consequently, these works often eschew efforts at non-partiality and objectivity and foreground the "selection, organization, diegesis, anecdote, temporal pacing, and emplotment" (Hutcheon 111) characterising the politics of historical knowledge and its representation.

The postmodern problematic that blurs the borderlines between fact and fiction, literature and history, spills over onto genres as well. Art Spiegelman, the author of *Maus*, expresses his consternation on seeing his graphic novel about the Holocaust placed among *The New York Times* bestseller list for *fiction*:

> If your list were divided into literature and nonliterature, I could gracefully accept the compliment as intended, but to the extent that 'fiction' indicates that a work isn't factual, I feel a bit queasy. . . .
>
> The borderland between fiction and nonfiction has been fertile territory for some of the most potent contemporary writing. . . . I shudder to think how David Duke – if he could read – would

respond to seeing a carefully researched work based closely on my father's memories of life in Hitler's Europe and in the death camps classified as fiction.

> I know that by delineating people with animal heads I've raised problems of taxonomy for you. Could you consider adding a special 'nonfiction/mice' category to your list? (qtd. in LaCapra 145)

What is abundantly evident in the question above is the sense of hybridity that characterises the postmodernist poetics whereby the borders between genres become difficult to demarcate. *Maus* is quite literally a survivor's tale that retells the trauma of the Holocaust in a graphic form. With its quasi-comic take on the Shoah – the genocide of Jews during the Second World War, an event that Spiegelman describes as the "central trauma of the Twentieth Century" (qtd. in LaCapra 140) – *Maus* is also a profoundly postmodernist representation of memory, history and representation itself.

Like several classic postmodernist texts, *Maus* combines qualities of different genres, emerging as an entanglement of biography, autobiography, memoir, graphic novel and animal fable. The anthropomorphic animals in *Maus* – where Jews are mice, Nazis are cats, Poles are pigs, French are frogs, Americans are dogs and Gypsies are moths – underline as well as subvert the stereotypes associated with these various races in popular discourse. While the graphic–comic form offers an artistic distance to Spiegelman as he retells the tale of a Holocaust survivor/storyteller, the author articulates the futility in the search for objective or absolute historical truth with the realisation that "essentially, the number of layers between an event and somebody trying to apprehend that event through time and intermediaries is like working with flickering shadows" (qtd. in Brown 98).

The metafictionality in Spiegelman's work is evident not just in the manner in which he draws attention to his narrative difficulty but also at a more fundamental level where he combines his animal allegory with the politics of representation. This is amply evinced in the novel in Artie's conversation with his wife Françoise about the nature of her animal symbolism in the novel:

> ARTIE: What kind of animal should I make you?
>
> FRANÇOISE: Huh? A mouse, of course!
>
> ARTIE: But you're French!
>
> FRANÇOISE: Well . . . How about the bunny rabbit?
>
> ARTIE: Nah, too sweet and gentle.
>
> FRANÇOISE: Hmmph.
>
> ARTIE: I mean the French in general. Let's not forget the centuries of anti-Semitism. . . . I mean, how about the Dreyfus affair? The Nazi collaborators! The—
>
> FRANÇOISE: Okay! But if you're a mouse, I ought to be a mouse too. I converted didn't I? (*Maus II* 11)

The passage combines several stereotypes drawing on popular historical knowledge as well as receptions of race in popular discourse while also being self-referential in the way it exhibits its constructed quality as a graphic-novel narrative in true postmodernist style. It also combines macro-narratives of history with personal whims and wishes that complicate any linear representation based on shared historical knowledge. The animal allegory and its associated iconography in *Maus*, far from being innocent artwork, is actually a testimony to the postmodernist historiographic metafiction – a form that is "provisional, continually reconstructed and open-ended" (Waugh 125) – that resists the rationale of hegemonic history through self-reflexive storytelling.

The metafictional character of *Maus* underlines the key qualities of formal deconstruction whereby Artie (the inset-storyteller who is a barely disguised version of Spiegelman himself) dramatises his own situatedness in the story he is trying to design, while also highlighting its ontological remove from the real world and its expected exchanges. This is made amply evident in the following exchange between Artie and his wife Françoise:

> ARTIE: Sigh. I feel so inadequate trying to reconstruct a reality that was worse than my darkest dreams. And trying to do it as a comic strip! I guess I bit off more than I can chew. Maybe I ought to forget the whole thing. There's so much I'll never be able to understand or visualize. I mean, reality is too complex for comics . . . so much has to be left out or distorted.
>
> FRANÇOISE: Just keep it honest, honey.
>
> ARTIE: See what I mean. In real life you'd never have let me talk this long without interrupting. (*Maus II* 16)

The metafictionality of the passage combines the anxiety and the politics of literary production with the anxiety of representing history – especially the horror of the Holocaust – in a faithful manner. It also underlines the supposed inadequacy of its generic location as a comic strip and accentuates the incongruity between lived life and a graphic novel. *Maus* combines comicality with trauma, relentlessly bastardising all the genres that it appropriates. It is quite literally a historiographic text and frequently plays with the allegorical and metaphorical tropes that it appears to assume. This is evinced in Artie's visit to his psychiatrist Pavel where he observes how the clinic is full of stray dogs and cats and wonders, "[c]an I mention this or does it completely louse up my metaphor?" (*Maus II* 43)

The location of the writer in *Maus* is also highlighted and dramatised by Spiegelman when in the chapter entitled "Auschwitz" the reader gets to see the mouse-mask falling off the human face of Artie, thus further dramatising the constructed quality of the self-reflexive historiographic metafiction. While being keenly aware that any representation of the history of the Holocaust is bound to be incomplete and inadequate – Artie lies on his therapist's couch and quotes Samuel Beckett's claim that "[e]very word is like an unnecessary stain on silence and nothingness" (qtd. in *Maus II* 45) – Spiegelman seems to suggest that it is still important to attempt a representation, albeit an unreliable and distorted one. *Maus* ends with Artie's father Vladek – the Holocaust survivor/storyteller in Spiegelman's graphic novel – asking Artie to turn off the recording tape, reclining in bed and exclaiming "I'm tired from talking Richieu, and it's enough stories for now" (*Maus II* 136). Vladek's use of the term "story" while narrating his history and horror of the Holocaust holds the key to the poetics of *Maus*. As a graphic novel about an un-narratable history of horror, *Maus* manages, as Hayden White argues, "to raise all of the crucial issues regarding the 'limits of representation' in general" ("Historical Employment" 42). This crisis of representation had been anticipated in Spiegelman's novel in the more existential crisis of traumatic memory whereby Vladek confessed to having burnt all of his wife Anja's diaries as "[t]hese papers had too many memories" (*Maus I* 158), much to the anger and consternation of his son Artie who wanted to design a narrative out of the horror that he himself had not experienced.

If the conclusion of *Maus* dramatises an exhaustion of stories and storytelling, with the dying Vladek urging Artie to stop his tape recorder while addressing him erroneously as Richieu, it is also a final dramatisation of the malleability of memory that emerges as an act of perverse yet productive preservation. The reader gets to know that Richieu happened to be Artie's brother who was killed during the Holocaust, a person whose story never got told. This instance of flawed memory and its entanglement with storytelling ironically emerges as the most appropriate ending for a postmodernist graphic novel about the trauma of genocide, one that situates self-conscious storytelling against the hegemony of history and forgetting alike. As a mimetically stylised representation of historical horror, Art Spiegelman's "image-text makes a good case against a dogmatic privileging of modernist techniques of estrangement and negation", showcasing through its historiography how "estrangement and affective mimesis are not mutually exclusive, but can actually reinforce each other" (Huyssen, "Of Mice and Mimesis" 82).

The plasticity and malleability of memory in *Maus* emerge as strategies to accommodate and articulate its traumatic quality, a trope Spiegelman re-uses in his post–9/11 graphic novel *In the Shadow of No Towers* (2004), where the Spiegelman–avatar appears in a page entitled "notes of a heartbroken narcissist", smoking a cigarette and staring blankly into a mirror, with the final panel-page in the sequence featuring Spiegelman in his *MAUS* avatar. The connection between the horrors of the Holocaust and that of 9/11 are made evident in Spiegelman's description of the indescribable quality of the air in Lower Manhattan and equating the same with his father's description of the smell of Auschwitz (3). If the metafictionality and intertextuality dramatised here are pointers to classic postmodernist poetics, as the two Spiegelman novels emerge as tellers of two major traumatic events in human history, *In the Shadow of No Towers* showcases the metonymic quality of consumerist life with Jihad appearing as a brand of footwear before becoming an acronym for political trauma post–9/11.

The literary texts examined above largely problematise the easy equation between hegemonic history, knowledge and identity by foregrounding the fictionality and constructed quality that underline such processes. They do so by highlighting their very own unreliability, incompletion and stylistic excesses embedded in their diegetic discourses. Both postmodernist historiographic metafiction and retellings of history dramatise the discursivity of historical knowledge and its politics of production. Like the hero of Angela Carter's *The Infernal Desire Machines of Doctor Hoffman* (1972) who is bewildered on discovering heavily varnished oil paintings in the wicked doctor's abode depicting "Leon Trotsky Composing the Eroica Symphony", Van Gogh writing *Wuthering Heights* and John Milton blindly executing "divine frescos upon the walls of the Sistine Chapel" (197–98), readers of these postmodernist works are deliberately jolted, shaken and shocked. The aim is not to escape the epistemic orders or the contexts of history but to offer alternative understandings of the nature of such orders and contexts. Placing private memories and fictional narratives above public knowledge and shared identities, postmodernist poetics dramatises the excesses of radical revisions and retellings. Such retellings often incorporate metafictional and narcissistic narratives situated against hegemonic orders of history and identity alike.

Works Cited

Amis, Martin. *Time's Arrow*. London: Jonathan Cape, 1991. Print.

Bakhtin, Mikhail. *The Dialogic Imagination: Four Essays*. Ed. Michael Holquist. Trans. Caryl Emerson and Michael Holquist. Austin, TX: U of Texas P, 1981. Print.

Bhabha, Homi K. *The Location of Culture*. New York: Routledge, 1994. Print.

Borges, Jorge Luis. "Borges and I." *Labyrinths*. Harmondsworth: Penguin Books, 1970. 246–47. Print.

Brown, Joshua. "Of Mice and Memory." *Oral History Review* 16.1 (Spring 1998): 91–109. Print.

Calvino, Italo. *If on a Winter's Night a Traveller*. Trans. William Weaver. New York: Harcourt Brace & Company, 1979. Print.

Carter, Angela. *The Infernal Desire Machines of Doctor Hoffman*. Harmondsworth: Penguin Books, 1972. Print.

Derrida, Jacques. *Archive Fever: A Freudian Impression*. Trans. Eric Prenowitz. Chicago, IL: U of Chicago P, 1998. Print.

---. *Of Grammatology*. Trans. Gayatri Chakravorty Spivak. Baltimore & London: John Hopkins UP, 1976. Print.

Doctorow, E. L. *Ragtime: A Novel.* New York: Random House, 1975. Print.

Foucault, Michel. *Language, Counter-Memory, Practice: Selected Essays and Interviews.* Trans. Donald F. Bouchard and Sherry Simon. Ithaca, NY: Cornell UP, 1977. Print.

---. *The Order of Things: An Archaeology of the Human Sciences.* New York: Pantheon Books, 1970. Print.

Fowles, John. *The French Lieutenant's Woman.* London: Jonathan Cape, 1969. Print.

Fuentes, Carlos. *Terranostra.* Harmondsworth: Penguin Books, 1978. Print.

Hutcheon, Linda. *A Poetics of Postmodernism.* New York & London: Routledge, 1988. Print.

Huyssen, Andreas. "Of Mice and Mimesis: Reading Spiegelman with Adorno." *New German Critique* 81 (Autumn 2000): 65–82. Print.

Kandel, Eric, and Larry Squire. *Memory: From Mind to Molecules.* Greenwood, CO: Roberts and Company, 2008. Print.

Kundera, Milan. *Testaments Betrayed: An Essay in Nine Parts.* Trans. Linda Asher. New York: HarperCollins, 1993. Print.

---. *The Book of Laughter and Forgetting.* Trans. Aaron Asher. New York: HarperCollins, 1996. Print.

LaCapra, Dominick. *History and Memory after Auschwitz.* Ithaca, NY: Cornell UP, 1998. Print.

Lucas, Rose. "The Parturition of Memory: Toni Morrison's 'Beloved'." *Australasian Journal of American Studies* 10.1 (July 1991): 39–47. Print.

Malabou, Catherine. *Plasticity at the Dusk of Writing: Dialectic, Destruction, Deconstruction.* Trans. Carolyn Shread. New York: Columbia UP, 2010. Print.

Man, Paul de. "Autobiography as De-Facement." *MLN* 94 (1979): 920–30. Print.

Márquez, Gabriel García. *Memories of My Melancholy Whores.* Trans. Edith Grossman. New York: Alfred A. Knopf, 2004. Print.

---. *One Hundred Years of Solitude*. Trans. Gregory Rabassa. New York: HarperCollins, 2003. Print.

McHale, Brian. *Postmodernist Fiction*. London: Methuen, 1987. Print.

Moglen, Helene. "Redeeming History: Toni Morrison's 'Beloved'." *Cultural Critique* 24 (Spring 1993): 17–40. Print.

Morrison, Toni. *Beloved*. New York: Alfred A. Knopf, 1987. Print.

Pynchon, Thomas. *Bleeding Edge*. New York: Penguin Press, 2013. Print.

Rushdie, Salman. "'Errata': or, Unreliable Narration in Midnight's Children." *Imaginary Homelands: Essays and Criticism 1981–1991*. New York: Penguin Books, 1992. 22–25. Print.

---. *Midnight's Children*. London: Vintage, 2012. Print.

---. *Shame*. New York: Random House, 2008. Print.

Sorrentino, Gilbert. *Imaginative Qualities of Actual Things*. New York: New Directions, 1971. Print.

Spiegelman, Art. *In the Shadow of No Towers*. New York: Viking Press, 2004. Print.

---. *Maus I: A Survivor's Tale: My Father Bleeds History*. New York: Pantheon Books, 1991. Print.

---. *Maus II: A Survivor's Tale: And Here My Troubles Began (From Mauschwitz to the Catskills and Beyond)*. New York: Pantheon Books, 1991. Print.

Waugh, Patricia. *Metafiction*. London: Routledge, 1984. Print.

White, Hayden. "Historical Emplotment and the Problem of Truth." *Probing the Limits of Representation: Nazis and the "Final Solution"*. Ed. Saul Friedlander. Cambridge, MA: Harvard UP, 1992. 37–53. Print.

---. "The Value of Narrativity in the Representation of Reality." *Critical Enquiry* 7.1 (Autumn 1980): 5–27. Print.

Notes

1. The theory of the nation as an imagined community was most famously propounded by Benedict Anderson and informs significant scholarship in postcolonial studies.
2. Freud appears also in D. M. Thomas's *The White Hotel* (1981), which is about the entanglement of erotic fantasies by one of Freud's patients and a chilling account of the Holocaust.
3. Chronotope, like carnivalesque, is a term theorised and popularised by Mikhail Bakhtin. As a form of epistemic as well as existential state, Bakhtin describes the chronotope as an "intrinsic connectedness of temporal and spatial relationships that are artistically expressed in literature" (84).

TWO

Postmodernism, Literature and Technology

"We are only telephone wires" (26)
—Rudyard Kipling[1]

Will Self's *Dorian: An Imitation* (2002) is a retelling of Oscar Wilde's *The Picture of Dorian Gray* (1890) with the 1980s gay scene and the hysteria around Princess Diana in the 1990s as its setting. Instead of the hand-drawn portrait in Wilde's novel, Self's story presents a video installation named *Cathode Narcissus* designed by the artist Baz Hallward concealed in an attic. In a remarkable retelling of Wilde's narrative of decadence and degeneration, Self's novel shows the AIDS-affected depravity suffered by the multiple screen images of the digital installation. Instead of the auratic artwork and its magical materiality in Wilde's novel, Dorian in Self's rendition is connected to a mutable machine and its simulacra on screen. The degeneration of the human self is thus reflected by an endlessly reproducible technology that digitises and dramatises a complex of depravity and downloadibility, the virtuality of the video becoming a pointer to the hyperreality of the increasingly prosthetic human self. Unsurprisingly, the "Epilogue" in *Dorian: An Imitation* constitutes a scene where the video *Cathode Narcissus* is embedded into a website (www.cathodenarcissus.com) that receives 2,456,707 hits in the month of May and whose homepage proclaims, "[d]ownload Some Perfection Today" (270).

Self's novel – an excellent example of intertextuality and metafictionality in relation to Wilde's original – dramatises certain key issues in the postmodernist entanglement of technology, fantasy and body. It showcases how the sense of self is not so much an apotheosis of unique organicity and embodied reality but a construct of virtual machines and their simulacra. The virtuality and mutability of the machines and their relationship to the human body are articulated powerfully in Jean Baudrillard's 1988 interview "The Work of Art in an Electronic Age", which extends as well as subverts Walter Benjamin's "The Work of Art in an Age of Mechanical Reproduction" in stating that "not only are there screens and terminals in technical terms, but we ourselves, the listeners, the TV spectators, become the terminals of all this communications network" (146). As a classic instantiation of Friedrich Kittler's analysis of how "[m]edia determine our situation" (xxxix), Self's *Dorian* describes the human being as a perfectly reducible and downloadable entity that is an extreme extension of Martin Heidegger's notion of the *standing-reserve* or *Bestand* aligned to an epistemic Enframing (*Ge-Stell*), whereby every energy can be converted into potentially passive recyclable order through the intervention of modern technology (17). In doing so, *Dorian* explores how the postmodern narrative manages to manoeuver outside biological essentialism and proffers a radical retelling of the feeling, living self as an extension of intuitive machines. More importantly, and at a fundamental level, Self's novel, like much of postmodern fiction and film, posits the ontological question concerning human beings' relation with technology: do human beings create technologies or do technologies create the human self? Instead of offering an easy answer, *Dorian: An Imitation* shows how the cellular materiality of human beings can be complexly aligned with the digital materiality of the virtual world in the twenty-first century technological imaginary.

Postmodernism's critique and revision of the metaphysics of presence spills over onto the process of writing itself, with perhaps its historic origin in the introduction of the typewriter that replaces the human hand. The discursive significance of the typewriter has been studied by several philosophers and cultural theorists, most notably by Martin Heidegger, who examined how typewriting tears the act of writing from the organic realm of the hand, and by Friedrich Kittler, who described the typewriter as a discursive machine gun with an operative mechanism similar to that of a revolver and a film projector (191). The violence embodied by the typewriter appears as early as in Bram Stoker's *Dracula* (1897) where the uncanny vampiric violence of the count is equated, among other things, with the technology of the typewriter. Perhaps the most penetrating critique of technology as it began to evolve at the turn of the twentieth century comes from Heidegger, who in his essay "The Question Concerning Technology" describes how modern machines operate on the principle of the standing-reserve, whereby everything, including human emotions and attributes, are endlessly reified and replicated for the purpose of productivity. The rule of Enframing, as examined by Heidegger, "threatens man with the possibility that it could be denied to him to enter into a more original revealing and hence to experience the call of a more primal truth" (28).

However, while Heidegger laments the loss of the purely organic, humanist essence of human beings in his increasing internalisation of technology, postmodernist poetics posits a more ambivalent and complex question around technology, viewing it as at once enslaving and emancipating. Essentially and functionally different from the Fordist and Taylorist principles of production that relied on centricity and sequentiality, postmodern technology relies instead on centrelessness whereby the real and the virtual orders are endlessly enmeshed together.

Nowhere is this shift from production to simulation, materiality to hyperreality examined more deeply than in the works of Jean Baudrillard who describes postmodernity as a permanent Disneyland – the "perfect model of all the entangled orders of simulation" (*Simulations* 23) – where surface ontologises substance through a play of fibres and phantasms.

Describing the relationship between the image and the real in terms of a transition through four phases, Baudrillard offers a trajectory along which the image travels and comes into being the way it does in the postmodern world. Thus, while in the first phase the image executes its fundamental mimetic function and offers a faithful reflection of reality, the second phase characterises the Marxist condition where the image becomes the bearer of mass culture and its emerging industry. In the second phase the image begins to assume an ideological function whereby basic reality begins to be masked. The third phase contains an ontological break in the image–real relationship in that the image begins to mask the absence of basic reality. The shift to the fourth phase sees the image generating itself for its own sake, as a pure simulacrum, with no resemblance whatsoever with any notion of reality. Describing the ontology of the hyperreal signifiers of postmodernity, Baudrillard underlines their representational imaginary thus:

> The real is produced from miniaturized units, from matrices, memory banks and command models – and with these it can be reproduced an indefinite number of times. It no longer has to be rational, since it is no longer measured against some ideal or negative instance . . . it is no longer real at all. It is a hyperreal: the product of an irradiating synthesis of combinatory models in a hyperspace without atmosphere. (*Simulations* 3)

Baudrillard's account above dramatises the movement of meanings and signs in the postmodern telos characterised by miniaturisation and multiplication, features that also mark much of postmodernist poetics. More significantly, and in keeping with the key tenets of posthumanism, postmodernist technology often blurs the borderlines between human and non-human, organic and inorganic, into an originless ontology perhaps best embodied in the figure of the cyborg.

Made famous in "A Cyborg Manifesto" (1984) by Donna Haraway, the figure of the cyborg appears to have been anticipated in an essay by Sigmund Freud where he describes the human as a prosthetic God at the turn of the twentieth century, surrounded by an endless network of machines, at once elevated and melancholy. Therefore, perhaps the most suitable way to study postmodern technology and its repercussions on literary narratives is to situate Freud as the foreseer of the cyborg. Examining the entanglement of human and machine around the turn of the twentieth century, Freud highlights the prosthetic and quasi-divine quality of the new human order while also observing the unhappiness that ensues despite the divinity triggered by technology:

> With every tool man is perfecting his own organs, whether motor or sensory, or is resolving the limits to their functioning. . . . Man has, as it were, become a kind of prosthetic God. When he puts on all his auxiliary organs he is truly magnificent; but those organs have not grown on to him and they still give him much trouble at times. . . in the interest of our investigations, we will not forget that present-day man does not feel happy in his God-like character. (737–38)

Like Heidegger, Freud here seems to view technology and the increasing internalisation of the same as the force that offers practical privileges while robbing humankind of its purely humanist position. The prosthetic God that the human becomes through technology is a pointer to the plasticity proffered by early-twentieth-century machines of mechanical reproduction such as the photograph, the radio and the gramophone. The mechanisation of humankind generates nervous discontents, according to Freud, with the network of machines emerging as a pointer to the network of neurosis mapping the early-twentieth-century metropolis. The prosthetic automatism characterises the melancholy, albeit wonderful, state of early-twentieth-century humans. However, the plastic prosthetic quality, as embodied by the cyborg, is frequently described by critical theorists as the most authentic example of postmodernist ambivalence. This is most substantially instantiated in the works of Donna Haraway.

Haraway's study of the cyborg inhabits the interstitial space between embodiment and appropriation, offering a compelling critique of patriarchy and phallogocentrism, one that emerges epistemologically aligned to the fundamental tenets of postmodernism. Emerging out of the Reagan-era of American capitalism, Haraway's "A Cyborg Manifesto" is a telling commentary on postmodern technology and is perhaps the most powerful example of the alliance between feminism and postmodernist poetics. Describing the cyborg as a "cybernetic organism, a hybrid of machine and organism, a creature of social reality as well as a creature of fiction" (150), Haraway elaborates on the machinic–mythic embodiment of such a state and its subversive potential. Far from decrying the cyborg-state as a loss of pure or organic humanism – thus establishing a discursive distance from the humanist nostalgia of Freud and Heidegger – Haraway celebrates its centrelessness in a true postmodernist spirit that situates itself against any Oedipal origin.

The cyborg emerges as an amalgam of the organic and the inorganic orders and interrogates established domains of family, patriarchy and the body, exemplifying a technological order designed to deconstruct. It appropriates a *technologic sublime* that far surpasses the Taylorist mode of production which seems *idyllic* in comparison. By pushing the patriarchal principle of production and amalgamation to its apocalyptic extreme, the cyborg subverts the same with an entanglement of illegitimacy and inauthenticity that emerges as an inconstant construct of a post–gender, post–production world. This is described by Haraway thus:

> The cyborg is a creature in a post-gender world; it has no truck with bisexuality, pre-Oedipal symbiosis, unalienated labour, or other seductions to organic wholeness. . . . In a sense, the cyborg has no origin story in the Western sense – a final' irony since the cyborg is also the awful apocalyptic telos of the 'West's' escalating dominations of abstract individuation, an ultimate self untied at last from all dependency, a man in space. (150–51)

Irreverent, incomplete and inconstant, the cyborg as described by Haraway is allied to the play between the signifier and the signified, between meaning and its opposite, a stylistic category recurrent in postmodernist aesthetics and fiction alike. As the "illegitimate offspring of militarism and patriarchal capitalism" (152), the cyborg breaks the borders between human and machine, human and animal, the real and the virtual.

Haraway's notion of the cyborg informs much of posthumanist theory subsequently, where the ontological divide between human and non-human orders blurs away in the face of the centreless technocracy emerging in the late-twentieth-century Western world. The posthumanist condition whereby human beings inhabit immersive technology and internalise the mechanism of intelligent and intuitive machines is powerfully portrayed in the works of theorists such as Rosi Braidotti and N. Katherine Hayles. Thus, Braidotti describes the symbiotic relationship between "the flesh and the machine" (223) in a culture where it is virtually impossible to distinguish "bodies from their technologically mediated extensions" (228). It is important to observe though that for Braidotti, as for many postmodernist theorists on technology, this immersion into a technologically-mediated embodiment offers opportunities to break away from the constraints of biological essentialism, and an alternative understanding of sexuality and body. This extension of the organic body into inorganic orders is further dramatised in the works of Katherine Hayles who, in *How We Became Posthuman* (1999), explores the entanglements between artificial intelligence, consciousness and embodiment in a culture where "synthetic sentience" is supplied on demand, determined by a "complex computational ecology in which many decisions, invisible to human attention, would be made by intelligent machines" (287). Elsewhere, in her provocatively titled *My Mother Was a Computer* (2005), Hayles examines a culture where "humans anthropomorphize the virtual creatures" and "virtual creatures computationalize the humans" (207), establishing a symbiotic relationship where man and machine blend different orders of embodiment and intelligence that cease to be disparate.

One of the finest and earliest examples in literature of humanity's embeddedness in a technological system that reifies as well as museum-ises human organic attributes is dramatised in Samuel Beckett's *Krapp's Last Tape* (1958). Beckett's one-act play about a sixty-nine-year-old decadent man desperately trying to remember and re-member his earlier selves through systematic recordings of his voice on his birthdays in a tape recorder, is a testimony to the blurring borderlines between organic and inorganic orders of recall, with the tape recorder replacing the human mind as a reservoir of memory. On his sixty-ninth birthday, instead of making the ritual recording, Krapp listens to the voice recorded on his thirty-ninth birthday and is subjected to a still silence at the end as the tape spools on as a symbol of his decanted self. The entanglement of biological and technological orders in *Krapp's Last Tape* has attracted the attention of posthumanist scholars such as Katherine Hayles, who states how the "play between the voices is an aural invitation to the audience to speculate on differences and similarities, across time and technology, even before the voices articulate words and sentences" ("Voices out of Bodies" 81).

Beckett's drama also instantiates Heidegger's notion of the endemic relation twentieth-century technology begins to form with nature, especially in ways such technology can bring forth an order of unconcealment that is, in essence, non-technological. The automatised quality of machinic memory and the human embeddedness in the same are dramatised in Beckett's play in Krapp's almost neurotic need to get a drink after each instance of recollection: "*gets up, goes backstage into darkness. Ten seconds. Pop of cork. Ten seconds. Second cork. Ten seconds. Third cork. Ten seconds. Brief burst of quavering song*" (218–19, italics in original). As Krapp's body mimics the mechanism of the recording machine, it also brings into play the body's plasticity across space and time as the thirty-nine-year-old Krapp reminiscing about his earlier self is aligned to the sixty-nine-year-old self doing the same.

As a "machine capable of replacing human communication with a prerecorded script" (Davidson 99), the tape recorder in *Krapp's Last Tape* also exteriorises the "phenomena in the skull" (Tajiri 161), thus dramatising a complex cacophony between the recording tape and the remembering mind. At once permanent and plastic, finite and elastic, the audiotapes in Beckett's play become pointers to identities that emerge across various vectors of space and time. The identities generated in tapes with recordings of Krapp commenting on earlier and younger avatars of himself bring forth the play between embodiment and machine-induced affect. This is instantiated when the recorded voice of the thirty-nine-year-old Krapp states, after having listened to "an old year", "[h]ard to believe I was ever that young whelp. The voice! Jesus! And the aspirations!" (218) A play where the "soundtrack of Krapp's life has become the life itself" (Albright 95), *Krapp's Last Tape* foregrounds a mutable machine meant as a reservoir of a dying self and is a curious revision of the Heideggerian Enframing, whereby the *bringing forth* emerges from an asymmetric entanglement of technology and the body.

The machinic materiality is also informed by an order of repeatability that characterises the human–non-human entanglement in Beckett's play, as instantiated in the observations Krapp manages to record in his final tape: "[l]ie propped up in the dark – and wander. Be again in the dingle on a Christmas Eve, gathering holly, the red-berried. [*Pause.*] Be again on Croghan on a Sunday morning, in the haze, with the bitch, stop and listen to the bells. [*Pause.*] And so on. [*Pause.*] Be again, be again" (223). The *being again* emerges as a complex of unique embodied subjectivity and repetitive technological virtuality as voices in a tape recorder. As an early example of the postmodernist play of mind, technology and agency, Beckett's play presents the self as a deconstructed text selectively and strategically embodying an extreme extension of the Heideggerian standing-reserve. Its historical significance lies in its minimalist depiction of man's embeddedness in an order of technology that appears limiting as well as liberating. Beckett's use of technology in *Krapp's Last Tape* and elsewhere in his oeuvre "attests to his historicisation of embodied experience" with the author "dedicating special attention to virtuality in his late television plays" (Maude 136). His last play, *What Where* (1983), presents posthuman ghosts that emerge after a technologically mediated eradication of the body. Beckett's writing may be considered as one of the first systematic attempts in literature to dramatise somatic, visceral and virtual experiences mediated through technology.

Perhaps the writer who happens to best anticipate and thematically shape the postmodernist poetics that underline the entanglement of technology and embodiment, machine and mind, is Thomas Pynchon, whose work also dramatises the counterculture emerging out of the political paranoia of the Cold War era. Equating war technology with the phallic principle of control, coercion and destruction, Pynchon's novels often exemplify the "total semiotechnology" that Friedrich Kittler describes as the site where everything, including life and death, takes place in the media that endlessly processes information ("Media and Drugs 159). Thus, Oedipa, the female protagonist of Pynchon's 1965 novel *The Crying of Lot 49*, finds herself stranded in an ontological divide between two mutually opposite orders of meaning, described thus with metaphors of information technology:

> It was now like walking among matrices of a great digital computer, the zeroes and ones twinned above, hanging like balanced mobiles right and left, ahead, thick, maybe endless. Behind the hieroglyphic streets there would either be a transcendent meaning, or only the earth. . . . Ones and zeroes. . . . Another mode of meaning behind the obvious, or none. (125–26)

Depicting a condition where the human is endlessly enmeshed in machinic modes of digitisation, Pynchon's novels anticipate the miniaturisation of data devices that often appear as orders of human embodiment. This is best instantiated in his 1973 novel *Gravity's Rainbow*, where data retrieval overdetermines all other human functions and where the protagonist Tyrone Slothrop is almost organically connected to a Second World War German V-2 rocket whose screams start the narrative of the novel which ends with a nose-diving rocket as well. *Gravity's Rainbow* describes a culture of constant surveillance wherein the protagonist is monitored from even before his birth by the "System" which includes a network of corporations such as Shell, General Electric, Krupp and IG Farben.

Gravity's Rainbow fictionalises the Heideggerian notion of Enframing whereby the individual is endlessly reified into becoming a productive entity monitored by a panoptical gaze. The "System" in Pynchon's novel operates by turning everything into a part of a profit principle and then converting bodies, vegetables and animals into a spectacle of used-up waste. The theatricality and virtuality of the war in *Gravity's Rainbow* are dramatised in an amphetamine-induced epiphany: "[t]his War was never political at all, the politics was all theatre all just to keep the people distracted . . . secretly, it was being dictated instead by the needs of technology . . . by a conspiracy between human beings and techniques, by something that needed the energy-burst of war" (617). Describing a condition where technology assumes an agency that overrides human will through the manufacturing and manipulation of simulated spectacles, *Gravity's Rainbow* appears to anticipate much of Baudrillard's work on war in the postmodern condition, especially his thesis on the Gulf War as an event that "makes its way by promotion and speculation, including the use of hostages transformed into marketing ploys", proceeding with a culture of concealment characterised by an absolute absence of "balance sheets, losses or operations" (*The Gulf War Did Not Take Place* 30).

A novel where conscious memory is triggered by "a soft and chemical smell, threatening, haunting" and unreal, and where the protagonist Tyrone Slothrop's sexual erection hums "like an instrument installed, wired by Them into his body as a colonial outpost" (300), *Gravity's Rainbow* depicts the endless entanglement of man and machine in a culture where the borderlines between violence and creation, production and annihilation, are permanently problematised. Pynchon's narrative inhabits the cusp where the panorama of technological sublime changes from being a totalitarian terror to a dark-humorous internalisation and is a particularly important novel in a historical study of technology and postmodernity. The war machine in Pynchon's novel appears to resonate with the totalitarian territorialisation of war machines described by Deleuze and Guattari, devices "installed in each hole, in every niche" (*A Thousand Plateaus* 214) in an absolute enactment of fascism. Crucially, *Gravity's Rainbow* also "articulates the affect particular to white male postmodernism" (McHugh 2) in its instantiation of human embeddedness in the automatism typical of capitalist patriarchy. Mixing stylistic elements from comedy, tragedy and slapstick typical of postmodernist poetics, *Gravity's Rainbow* dramatises white countercultural politics in post–Cold War America and in the process showcases the limits of representation itself.

The postmodernist critique in Pynchon's novel is directed against the science that historically informed European Enlightenment, caricatured in *Gravity's Rainbow* in the institution entitled PISCES (Psychological Intelligence Schemes for Expediting Surrender) headed by the figure of Ned Pointsman, who is a self-proclaimed admirer of Pavlov and appropriates a vision of the world that operates on the binary of stimulus and response, on and off, effect and cause. A grotesque parody of the dualism of Western Enlightenment, PISCES operates as an all-seeing all-encompassing organisation concerned with a "strictly defined, clinical version of truth" (324) with no wider agency. Against such a totalitarian, technocratic regime, Pynchon's novel situates the counterculture embodied by the protagonist Tyrone Slothrop, whose sites of sexual adventures align perfectly with the sites where the Rocket lands in the map of London. The resonance between Slothrop's sexual state and the phallic quality of the Rocket is further corroborated by the plastic Imoplex G used on the infant Slothrop to achieve erection as well as being the key element constituting the Rocket's manual. In true postmodernist fashion, the Rocket and Slothrop's association with the same become at once dystopian and liberating, the quest for discovering the man–machine entanglement also becoming a means to escape the totalitarian terror embodied by Pointsman and PISCES.

The countercultural resistance enacted by Slothrop in *Gravity's Rainbow* – as he joins hands with the other revolutionaries in the German Zone – is largely libidinal, culminating in an orgy on the *Anubis*, a ship hosting porn stars and European royalty together in various sexual states, a perfect example of the postmodern entanglement where high-culture and kitsch, the elevated and the decadent inhabit one platform of pastiche. A novel where the "centrality of plastic indicates the power of human discourse to shape material reality at a molecular level" (McHugh 5), *Gravity's Rainbow* is essentially about the plasticity of identities in a postmodern multiverse where "machines chatter and ring to each other" (*Gravity's Rainbow* 299). In the true spirit of postmodern poetics, Pynchon's novel combines symbols of procreation and annihilation, most iconically with a "wirephoto of a giant white cock, dangling in the sky straight downward out of a white pubic bush" (822) with its associated image of phallic procreation as well as being reminiscent of the mushroom clouds born out of the Hiroshima atom bomb.

Gravity's Rainbow is a novel that celebrates the counterforce against totalitarian terror while also underlining the limits of resistance in a postmodern world where any form of counterculture eventually emerges as part of the dominant discourse of control and coercion. The final image in the novel – depicting a Nazi Rocket shot in 1945 falling on a 1970 film theatre – brings the entanglement of postmodernism, technology and historical time into a compelling climax with the spectre of fascism symbolically invading the post–Cold War culture industry and its simulated identities. In its depiction and dramatisation of shared simulacra and visual violence, *Gravity's Rainbow* appears to anticipate the post–9/11 technologically designed desert of the real that, as Slavoj Žižek states, is a "discursive product, a symbolic fiction which we misperceive as a substantial autonomous entity" (*Welcome to the Desert of the Real!* 19).

The blurred borderlines between space and time, human and non-human, and real and virtual, permeate much of postmodernist fiction where technology often appears as an alienating apparatus that problematises human sentience and agency alike. Paul Virilio's works in the 1990s are testament to this culture of writing, perhaps best exemplified in *Open Sky* (1997) which depicts an order of teletechnology that acts as a man–machine interface whose interactivity is as dangerous as radioactivity. Virilio describes a world where automatism and instantaneity blur the divisions between subjects and objects while also affecting the order and agency of human self-realisation. Likewise, Don DeLillo's 2003 novel *Cosmopolis* shows how the city of New York produces human subjectivities through a network of machines including a constantly functional spycam, screens monitoring heartbeats, telescreens inside a limousine and an electronic camera embedded in a wristwatch, in an entanglement of machinic materiality and affective nostalgia where a character confesses, "cash machines have a charisma that still speaks to me" (60). The protagonist Eric Parker, a multimillionaire trader who inhabits "the intersection between technology and capital" (23), journeys across New York city in his white limousine wearing a bulletproof jacket experiencing an anti-capitalist riot, a funeral, a medical checkup and a haircut. In essence, Parker becomes an embodiment of Freud's prosthetic God who ends up being melancholy and kills himself despite his quasi-divine status, even as he watches his own death on his wristwatch camera before he actually dies, and says "O shit I'm dead.... He'd always wanted to become quantum dust" (206). The theme of death mediated by technology occurs also in DeLillo's *White Noise* (1985) where death and disaster are disseminated as SIMUVAC (Simulated Evacuation) that precedes and overdetermines organic apperception.

DeLillo's *Cosmopolis* highlights the historicity of the technology that surrounds and often determines the human body and its movements, while also underlining the epistemic order it entails. One such instance in *Cosmopolis* occurs thus:

> He was thinking about automated teller machines. The term was aged and burdened by its own historical memory. It worked at cross-purposes, unable to escape the inference of fuddled human personnel and jerky moving parts. The term was part of the process that the device was meant to replace. It was anti-futuristic, so cumbrous and mechanical that even the acronym seemed dated. (54)

Cosmopolis dramatises a dystopia that is futuristic as well as contemporary, showcasing how the act of living entails embeddedness in a world of velocity and machines whose movements are barely noticeable even as they permeate and produce human subjectivity. This is articulated in *Cosmopolis* by the character Vija Kinski who juxtaposes ancient Chinese wisdom with the Western metropolitan order:

> . . . it's all random phenomena. You apply mathematics and other disciplines, yes. But in the end you're dealing with a system that's out of control. Hysteria at high speeds, day to day, minute to minute. People in free societies don't have to fear the pathology of the state. We create our own frenzy, our own mass convulsions, driven by thinking machines that we have no final authority over. The frenzy is barely noticeable most of the time. It's simply how we live. (85)

An entanglement of emotions and machines characterise the narrative of *Cosmopolis* where Karl Marx's famous quote about the haunting spectre of capitalism appears at the top tier in an electronic display screen. It is a state where man manufactures machines that in turn manufacture emotions and affect, enacting an endless loop of frenzy and phenomena in a cityspace that may be described using Edward Soja's notion of the "postmetropolis", where the urban imaginary is intimately linked to "postfordist economic restructuring, intensified globalization, . . . the deterritorialization and reterritorialization of cultures and identity" (324). The metropolis in DeLillo's novel instantiates Henri Lefèbvre's notion of "the production of space" that can be subjectively experienced as well as empirically classified. It is a centreless site where abstraction and materiality are ultimately underpinned by the codes of a capitalist culture (36–46). The overdetermination of the capital is evinced in *Cosmopolis* even in the anti-capitalist riot, as the rioters "don't exist outside the market", which produces the chilling knowledge that "[t]here is no outside" (90).

Cosmopolis creates a space that generates identities as well as its simulated opposites, where "[s]urface, surface, surface was all that anyone found meaning in" (375) as stated by Patrick Bateman, the handsome Wall Street investment banker who becomes a psychotic serial killer at night in Bret Easton Ellis's 1991 novel *American Psycho*. It also corresponds to Jean Baudrillard's description of the coded quality of the technocratic postmodern city and the endless reproducibility and artificiality of the postmodern urban imaginary ("Kool Killer" 76–86) that is described as the "mythical . . . cyber-capital" (207) in DeLillo's novel. Baudrillard's essay examines the endless dissemination of signs and superficial signifiers that are technologically mediated, integrating as well as disintegrating identity in the postmodern metropolis. This is dramatised in Paul Auster's *Travels in the Scriptorium* (2006) where an old man, frustrated by the endlessness of surface signs, exclaims, "[w]hen is this nonsense going to end?", only to receive a response from the narrator, "[i]t will never end" (143).

If *Cosmopolis* exhibits the embodiment of hyperreality in the postmodern metropolis, the notion of the cyberspace as a technologically mediated site of epistemic exchange receives its first full treatment in William Gibson's classic *Neuromancer* (1984), which describes cyberspace as a ". . . consensual hallucination experienced daily by billions of legitimate operators, in every nation, by children being taught mathematical concepts. . . . A graphical representation of data abstracted from the banks of every computer in the human system. Unthinkable complexity. Lines of light ranged in the non-space of the mind, clusters and constellations of data. Like city lights, receding . . ." (67). Gibson's novel – a cyberpunk narrative with a cult following – is about the dimensionless and locationless quality of the postmodern techno-cosmos that merges with the subjectivity of the human mind, creating space and nonspace alike. It also exhibits the uneasy alliance and interchangeability between natural organic intelligence and artificial inorganic intelligence (embodied in the novel by Wintermute and Neuromancer), between deadness and digital reproduction (exemplified by the character "Flatline" McCoy Pauley) and between natural humans and digital databases (exemplified by Case, the protagonist of the novel). With an opening sentence that equates the sky above a port with the "color of television, tuned to a dead channel", and which describes a bartender who fills glasses with a prosthetic arm and smiles showing teeth that are "a webwork of East European steel and brown decay" (1), Gibson's *Neuromancer* is a profoundly postmodern and posthuman novel that transgresses the notional binaries between the real and the virtual.

Neuromancer dramatises the ontological randomness in a hyper-technologised world where real characters (Armitage/Corto) are eventually revealed as having been built by computer programmes, where the protagonist Case "keys" into the sensorium of the prostitute Molly, "into the sinuous flow of muscle, senses sharp and bright" (72), via a "simstim" switch and where human memory emerges "unreeled with the monotony of an unedited simstim tape" (151). It showcases a condition where the medium of communication determines the location and the very existence of human identity, corroborating Baudrillard's examination of how "being is convertible into infinite forms, and values of identity are constituted primarily through the manipulation of technology" ("The Work of Art in an Electronic Age" 145). *Neuromancer* follows the story of a "cyberspace cowboy" named Case who is "a byproduct of youth and proficiency, jacked into a custom cyberspace deck that projected his disembodied consciousness into the consensual hallucination that was the matrix" (12) (the global representation of the databases of all computers in the human system). The novel is also a significant narrative about biotechnology in a posthuman world where any organ can be planted as well as supplanted in any body from anywhere else, and where human organic matter appears as "a flat lozenge of vatgrown flesh that lay on a carved pedestal of imitation jade" (23). It is a world that witnesses "data made flesh in the mazes of the black market" (26) and where a prostitute carries lethal foldable blades buried under her fingernails embodying a complex amalgam of human and machine, desire and death.

The postmodern cyberpunk, as exemplified by Gibson's *Neuromancer* and other similar works, dramatises a defamiliarised order peopled by perverts, cyborgs and psychopaths. In doing so, it lays bare a "cognitive mapping" structured to "find a suitable means for displaying the powerful and troubling technological logic that underlines the postmodern condition", while also exhibiting through a unique technical craftsmanship some of the most fundamental existential problems about the nature of reality and human identity (McCaffrey 16). The themes of alternative avatars and the plastic production of identities are also dramatised in George Alec Effinger's trilogy *When Gravity Fails* (1987), *A Fire in the Sun* (1989) and *The Exile Kiss* (1991), where injected software in wired brains determines personality patterns ("moddies") that are easily purchasable from "modshops". Effinger describes a mercilessly stratified world where members of the poorer populace are routinely killed in order to supply organs to the richer citizens who can afford to pay, thus generating a black market of body parts available to the wealthy. Likewise, human emotions emerge as perfectly downloadable through systematic torture and can be stored for sale subsequently. The theme of mind–software entanglement appears in Walter Jon Williams's 1986 novel *Hardwired*, where a powerful programme entitled Project Black Mind selects, supplants and superimposes human minds and their associated attributes. A similar theme appears in Pat Cadigan's *Mindplayers* (1987), where humans are able to purchase artificial identities from Power People company and are subject to censorship by the Brain Police that has the ability to wipe out entire personalities and traits through a mechanism called "mindsuck".

As a stylistic genre, cyberpunk fiction exemplifies, in the words of Fredric Jameson, "the impossible totality of the contemporary world system" by exhibiting an "exceptional literary realization" that alchemises technology into fictional narratives (38). In the process, it extends the postmodernist style of *covert narcissistic narration* that proceeds with disruption and discontinuity, drawing attention to the constructed quality of the story itself that emerges as an artifice (Hutcheon 141). Along with offering a stylised critique of technocratic dystopias and describing the human embeddedness in such discourse networks, the postmodern cyberpunk often highlights the anxieties of the racial, cultural and political marginalia. As Dick Hebdige argues, the postmodern punk frequently emerges as an excessive appropriation of non-white ethnicities and aesthetics, positioning itself against "fat businessmen" and "lard-ass capitalists" (64). Gibson's *Neuromancer* alludes to such themes by pointing at the prospective demise of white colonialism and control, referred to in the novel as "Babylon". In another of his works titled *Mona Lisa Overdrive* (1988) Gibson problematises the notion of memory and hegemonic history by entangling it with the automatism and plasticity of machines, embodied in the figure of Colin who reconstructs London's hidden history through a process of simulation in virtual vehicles. The perfectibility and plasticity of such machines are manifested in the degree of defamiliarisation they achieve on the gendered subject, as evident in the posthuman prostitute Molly in *Neuromancer* and the "[s]lavic Barbies", the prostitutes who achieve "assembly-line beauty" (Gibson, *Idoru* 3) through plastic surgery in the Kafka club in Gibson's *Idoru* (1996).

The entanglement of technology and the human body is also dramatised in Angela Carter's *The Passion of New Eve* (1977) that describes "a complicated mix of mythology and technology" (44), while also bringing in complexities of gender in a post-apocalyptic America marked by war zones where Blacks battle whites. However, Carter's most unsettling account of human–machine interface is presented in her 1972 novel *The Infernal Desire Machines of Doctor Hoffman* that showcases a sinister attempt to "base a meta-technology upon metaphysics only by the most scrupulous observance of and adherence to the laws of empirical research" (259). In her introduction to the novel, Ali Smith describes Carter's novel as an "imagistically cornucopic and virtuoso performance" that emerges as a "visionary book for a virtual age" (viii). An intertextual parody of the German Romantic E.T.A. Hoffmann's tales, Carter's *The Infernal Desire Machines of Doctor Hoffman* is a profoundly postmodernist work that is a critique of super-scientific patriarchy and makes allusions to works such as Proust's *À la recherche du temps perdu* (1871–1922) in its rendition of remembering and forgetting as functions of existential sustenance. Carter's novel, with its map of machines that generate desire and death alike, poses key questions about the ontology of reality in an age of virtual vehicles.

A novel where "the freak is the norm" (130) and where desiring machines are designed to distort reality, *The Infernal Machines of Doctor Hoffman*, like Martin Amis's *Yellow Dog* (2003), shows how "obscenification" and "scientification" often inhabit the same ontological plane (Crews 649). In describing a city besieged by a diabolical doctor who generates guerrilla minions, unreal invaders emerging out of "amorphous spooks" (*The Infernal Desire Machines* 4) from fissures in mirrors, Carter presents her protagonist Desiderio, the war hero and survivor of an onslaught against reason. The novel depicts a world where humans carry out machinic functions and attributes alike, as exemplified in the figure of Nao-Kurai's mother whom Desiderio calls Mama, who, like all other women, "moved in the same stereotyped way, like benign automata" (82). The diabolical doctor, who attempts to distort reality with his desire machines, eventually emerges "as weightless as a doll" (264) in the final fight that culminates in the doctor's death, followed by the death of his daughter Albertina, who, like the doctor himself, is killed by Desiderio who also happened to love her.

The desire machines in Carter's novel – complex automata that defamiliarise reality – emerge as an extension of the "little schizo machines of becoming-god or becoming-beetle" (Deleuze and Guattari, *A Thousand Plateaus* 34) that Deleuze and Guattari describe as the epiphenomena of a schizophrenic capitalist culture. Describing desire machines as complex and endless assemblages of automatic and embodied orders, Deleuze and Guattari examine their process of ontologisation:

> [o]nce the structural unity of the machine has been undone, once the personal and specific unity of the living has been laid to rest, a direct link is perceived between the machine and desire, the machine passes to the heart of desire, the machine is desiring and desire, machined. Desire is not in the subject, but the machine in desire – with the residual subject off to the side, alongside the machine, around the entire periphery, a parasite of machines, an accessory of vertebro-machinate desire. (*Anti-Oedipus* 285)

The passage above dramatises the blurred borderlines between automatism and desire, locating the latter in the heart of desire itself. What is emphasised – and this is in keeping with the postmodernist tendency towards technology apropos of artistic activities – is the increasing humanisation and internalisation of the machinic quality that becomes an organic part of the human nervous system. The feverish quality of Carter's *Infernal Desire Machines of Doctor Hoffman* – where the diabolical doctor fills a city with mirages to drive all citizens mad – corresponds to Deleuze and Guattari's descriptions in *Anti-Oedipus* of a world of endlessly interconnected machines where human subjects are generated as residuum or appendix adjacent to machinic movements (20). Describing a work of art as a desiring machine in itself, Deleuze and Guattari highlight the blurring borderlines between human and machine – a theme that runs throughout Carter's *Infernal Desire Machines* along with an entanglement of memory and amnesia. As Michel Foucault examines in his preface to *Anti-Oedipus*, the analysis by Deleuze and Guattari highlights the *schizophrenic process of desire* that in turn captures the movements from "paranoia to schizophrenia, from fascism to revolutions, from breakdowns to breakthroughs" (xvii).

What the novels examined above largely describe – and this is in keeping with the postmodern poetics of excess and entanglements – is the endless embeddedness of the human system in a world of machines that blur the borders between the real and the virtual. While Pynchon's novels dramatise technology as an overseeing presence that compromises and eventually enervates the human will to change, the more recent novels of Gibson and DeLillo offer a more ambivalent attitude towards the human–machine interface. The miniaturisation and digitisation of technology and the human mimicry of the same as depicted in postmodern novels are often reflective of the aleatory quality of the world we inhabit. Frequently foreboding while also being darkly humorous, postmodern fiction that deals with human–technology entanglements examines the limits of liberation and the uneasy alliance between resistance and re-appropriation, often inspiring other art forms such as music, painting and cinema. Largely indicative of the looseness and plasticity of existence in a world where the human body and the self can be converted into endlessly downloadable entities with their special simulated identities, postmodern fiction about technology also underlines the machinic quality of "pure" human attributes such as emotions, affect and memory. Far from creating the melancholy quasi-God with his prosthetic embodiment as described by Freud, postmodern technology moves away from the binaries of human/non-human and organic/inorganic, and in the process pushes towards a naturalisation of the cyborg-state.

While on the one hand, postmodern technology as depicted in major works of fiction requires a special skill-set in order to operate, on the other it also offers a form of social levelling whereby older orders of human and social supremacy (especially gendered and racialised) begin to blur away in the effort to appropriate artificiality. More importantly, the increasing digitisation of information and knowledge that characterises postmodern technology (and its representations in literature) often playfully problematises the difference between "true" information and "false" information, in perfect correspondence with the postmodern plasticity informing "real" identities and virtual identities, between objective ontology and simulated spectacles which are consumed ad nauseam. With its entanglement of showmanship and surveillance, censorship and spectacle, postmodern technology often exhibits an immersive quality that entails an annihilation of the pure organic order even as it constructs inauthentic epistemic orders that are selectively subversive in their ontology and functionality. As the novels discussed above depict, this postmodern plasticity in technology extends into the domain of bioscience as well, with the human body and mind frequently emerging as mutable machines connected to artificial support systems that often operate like Deleuzean rhizomes that are incomplete as well as infinite. Historically, the invention of biomedical technology such as artificial insemination – with the first test tube baby Louise Brown born in England in 1978 – genetic screening and genetic engineering – with the first cloned creature, Dolly the sheep, created in 1996 – ushered in public euphoria as well as paranoia with its mechanism of multiplicity and simulated identities. On the one hand, there was the possibility of alternate procreation that could subvert biological inabilities, on the other, laboratory births and the concept of designer babies fuelled dystopian fears about an unnatural species of humanity that was an extreme extension of neoliberal reification. The test tube baby quickly became a metaphor for technologised procreation that redressed biological inadequacy, as well as of machinic reproduction that undermined human agency and may be regarded as a symbolic site for postmodernism's ambivalence about technology.

The genetic manipulations, plastic permutations and anatomical extensions that characterise twenty-first–century biomedicine may be considered as epiphenomena of the entanglement of invisibility and spectacle that broadly underlines postmodernist technology. Crucially, such extensions and simulations compromise as well as alleviate the agency of the human subject who often emerges as the viewer as well as the viewed in the tragicomic telos of postmodern existence.

The *information economy* that emerged from the 1990s in the Western world with the boom of the dot-com, may be considered a major signifier of postmodern technology that operated on principles distinctly different from earlier politics of production that relied on manufacturing and maintenance. The Internet, with its deluge of digitised identities and simulated spectacles, fundamentally shifted the ontology of technology from the Heiddegerian standing-reserve to a centreless and infinitely distributive network, where the high and the low, the profound and the pastiche, are all endlessly enmeshed, like the ship-deck in Pynchon's *Gravity's Rainbow*. Like the rootless rhizomes described by Deleuze as an assemblage of living machines, postmodern technology – exemplified by the Internet – shifted the structure of knowledge from its organic, physical and humanist roots to a plastic and playful platform where knowledge becomes information that can be endlessly deconstructed as well as reconstructed. The ambivalent attitude towards technology – as instantiated in many postmodern novels like those examined above – is also reflected more specifically in the general reaction to twentieth–century physics. While Einsteinian relativity ushered in new possibilities of knowledge, of plastic space and time which was a major influence on contemporary art forms such as Picasso's Cubism as well as on unreliable and multifocal postmodern fiction, with *E = mc2* becoming a slogan on T-shirts as well as in academic conferences, the permanent paranoia generated by the atom bombs dropped at Nagasaki and Hiroshima fuelled fears of technologic destruction of apocalyptic proportions.

The postmodern poetics of virtuality and simulated identities spills over onto popular media as well, most evidently in Hollywood films such as Peter Weir's *The Truman Show* (1998) and The Wachowski Brothers's *The Matrix* trilogy (1999–2003) that deliberately celebrate the simulacra generated out of "pure" human belief and body. These works of cinema, like the works of literature examined above, describe the defamiliarised difference between lived reality and spectacular virtuality, while also showcasing how an increasing internalisation of the latter informs the state of the former in postmodernity. Like the state of Truman Burbank in Weir's film and that of Neo in *The Matrix* trilogy, postmodern human existence is almost entirely simulated and spectacular, where consumers become the consumed in an endless loop of hyperreality and commodity. If anything, such films show how the borderlines between the biological human and the simulated cyborg become increasingly tenuous in an age of deathless digitisation. As with everything else, postmodern fiction about technology and technologisation explores the ambivalent articulation of fear and freedom, of paranoia and possibility, which are often simultaneously embodied and experienced.

Works Cited

Albright, Daniel. *Beckett and Aesthetics*. Cambridge: Cambridge UP, 2003. Print.

Auster, Paul. *Travels in the Scriptorium*. New York: Picador, 2006. Print.

Baudrillard, Jean. "Kool Killer, or, The Insurrection of Signs." *Symbolic Exchange and Death*. London: Sage, 1993. 76–86. Print.

---. *Simulations*. Trans. Paul Foss, Paul Patton and Philip Beitchman. New York: Semiotext, 1983. Print.

---. *The Gulf War Did Not Take Place.* Trans. Paul Patton. Bloomington, IN: Indiana UP, 1995. Print.

---. "The Work of Art in an Electronic Age." Trans. Lucy Forsyth. *Baudrillard Live: Selected Interviews.* Ed. Mike Gane. London & New York: Routledge, 1988. 145–51. Print.

Beckett, Samuel. "Krapp's Last Tape." *Complete Dramatic Works.* London: Faber and Faber, 1986. 213–24. Print.

Braidotti, Rosi. *Metamorphosis: Towards a Materialist Theory of Becoming.* Cambridge: Polity, 2002. Print.

Carter, Angela. *The Infernal Desire Machines of Doctor Hoffman.* London: Penguin Books, 2011. Print.

---. *The Passion of New Eve.* London: Virago, 1982. Print.

Crews, Brian. "Martin Amis and the Postmodern Grotesque." *The Modern Language Review* 105.3 (July 2010): 641–59. Print.

Davidson, Michael. "Technologies of Presence: Orality and the Tapevoice of Contemporary Poetics." *Sound States: Innovative Poetics and Acoustical Technologies.* Ed. Adalaide Morris. Chapel Hill & London: U of North Carolina P, 1997. 97–125. Print.

Deleuze, Gilles, and Félix Guattari. *A Thousand Plateaus: Capitalism and Schizophrenia.* Trans. Brian Massumi. Minneapolis: U of Minnesota P, 1987. Print.

---. *Anti-Oedipus.* Trans. Robert Hurley. Minneapolis: U of Minnesota P, 1983. Print.

DeLillo, Don. *Cosmopolis: A Novel.* New York & London: Scribner, 2003. Print.

Ellis, Bret Easton. *American Psycho.* London: Picador, 1991. Print.

Foucault, Michel. Preface. *Anti-Oedipus.* By Gilles Deleuze and Félix Guattari. Trans. Robert Hurley. Minneapolis: U of Minnesota P, 1983. Print.

Freud, Sigmund. "Civilization and Its Discontents." *The Freud Reader.* Ed. Peter Gay. London: W. W. Norton & Company, 1989. 722–71. Print.

Gibson, William. *Idoru.* London: Penguin Books, 1996. Print.

---. *Neuromancer.* London: Victor Gollancz Ltd, 1984. Print.

Haraway, Donna. "A Cyborg Manifesto: Science, Technology and Socialist-Feminism in the Late Twentieth Century." *Simians, Cyborgs and Women: The Reinvention of Nature*. New York: Routledge, 1991. 149–81. Print.

Hayles, N. Katherine. *How We Became Posthuman: Virtual Bodies in Cybernetics, Literature and Informatics*. Chicago & London: U of Chicago P, 1999. Print.

---. *My Mother Was a Computer: Digital Subjects and Literary Texts*. Chicago & London: U of Chicago P, 2005. Print.

---. "Voices out of Bodies, Bodies out of Voices: Audiotape and the Production of Subjectivity." *Sound States: Innovative Poetics and Acoustical Technologies*. Ed. Adalaide Morris. Chapel Hill & London: U of North Carolina P, 1997. 74–96. Print.

Hebdige, Dick. *Subculture: The Meaning of Style*. London & New York: Methuen, 1988. Print.

Heidegger, Martin. *The Question Concerning Technology and Other Essays*. Trans. William Lovitt. New York: Harper & Row, 1977. Print.

Hutcheon, Linda. *Narcissistic Narrative: The Metafictional Paradox*. Waterloo, Ontario: Wilfrid Laurier UP, 1980. Print.

Jameson, Fredric. *Postmodernism: Or the Cultural Logic of Late Capitalism*. Durham, NC: Duke UP, 1991. Print.

Kipling, Rudyard. *Traffics and Discoveries*. Harmondsworth: Penguin Books, 1987. Print.

Kittler, Friedrich. Preface. *Gramophone, Film, Typewriter*. Trans. Geoffrey Winthrop-Young and Michael Wutz. Stanford, CA: Stanford UP, 1999. xxxix–xli. Print.

---. "Media and Drugs in Pynchon's Second World War." *Reading Matters: Narratives in the New Media Ecology*. Trans. Michael Wutz and Geoffrey Winthrop-Young. Ed. Joseph Tabbi and Michael Wutz. Ithaca, NY & London: Cornell UP, 1997. 157–72. Print.

Lefèbvre, Henri. *The Production of Space*. Trans. Donald Nicholson-Smith. Oxford: Blackwell, 1991. Print.

McCaffrey, Larry. "Introduction: The Desert of the Real." *Storming the Reality Studio: A Casebook of Cyberpunk and Postmodern Science Fiction*. Ed. Larry McCaffrey. London & Durham, NC: Duke UP, 1991. 1–16. Print.

Maude, Ulrika. *Beckett, Technology and the Body*. Cambridge: Cambridge UP, 2009. Print.

McHugh, Patrick. "Cultural Politics, Postmodernism, and White Guys: Affect in *Gravity's Rainbow*." *College Literature* 28.2 (Spring 2001): 1–28. Print.

Pynchon, Thomas. *Gravity's Rainbow*. London: Viking, 1973. Print.

---. *The Crying of Lot 49*. London: Vintage Classics, 1996. Print.

Self, Will. *Dorian: An Imitation*. London: Penguin, 2003. Print.

Smith, Ali. Introduction. *The Infernal Desire Machines of Doctor Hoffman*. By Angela Carter. London: Penguin, 2010. vii–xii. Print.

Soja, Edward W. *Postmetropolis: Critical Studies of Cities and Regions*. Malden, MA: Blackwell, 2000. Print.

Tajiri, Yoshiki. *Samuel Beckett and the Prosthetic Body: The Organs and Senses in Modernism*. London: Palgrave Macmillan, 2007. Print.

Žižek, Slavoj. *Welcome to the Desert of the Real!: Five Essays on September 11 and Related Dates*. London: Verso, 2002. Print.

Notes

1. Kipling wrote this to Ryder Haggard in 1904 while also writing a short story entitled "Wireless" in 1902, which dramatises an entanglement of telegraphic and telepathic communication whereby an apothecary's assistant channelises Keats's poem "The Eve of St. Agnes" in a semi-wakeful state with a spiritual séance with the poet.

THREE

Postmodernism, Gender and Performativity

Christa Wolf's story "Selbstversuch" ("Self-Experiment") – written in 1972 in Communist East Germany but set twenty years later in 1992 – presents a scene where a female scientist participates in a biochemical experiment on sex change and breaks off in the middle of the experiment in order to compose a critical scientific report on the same (201–05). In Wolf's story, the female protagonist injects an experimental drug named *Petersein Masculinum 199* into her system that transforms her into a man named Anders. The narrative reveals how the protagonist is forced to forsake her female identity in order to appropriate the cutting-edge quality of bioscientific research as a scientist. Unsurprisingly, Anders, the engineered male self generated out of the sex-change experiment, loses the ability to speak in a symbolic depiction of the crisis of agency suffered by the woman in order to embody and enact the extended phallogocentric desire of medical science. Crucially, Anders realises that the loss of female breasts is less significant in terms of negotiating with the new gender identity than the absence of the male gaze, in a telling entanglement of biomedically and discursively produced gender identities (221).

By "deconstructing gender as an epistemological category" (Hermann 53),[1] Wolf's "Self-Experiment" situates the existential self with its many memories against the empirical self engineered by a biochemical experiment and describes how the change of gender brings about a conflict of male and female identities, symbolically embodied by the space of the

Niemandsland (No man's land) in the story. "Self-Experiment" ends with the protagonist abandoning the sex-change experiment, choosing her old organic self and producing a critical medical report on the experiment. This is done at the behest of the protagonist's male professor who feels threatened when the biomedically engineered "male" Anders begins to date his daughter. The experiment comes to an end at the precise moment when the narrator regains her voice and the story begins, in a telling convergence of corporeality and narrative agency.

Wolf's story – now considered as one of the early examples of feminist cyborg fiction (Eigler 11)[2] – is pregnant with the possibilities and precarious constructions and deconstructions of gender identities in social, professional and epistemic orders (the very act of becoming a medical scientist and appropriating the masculinist rationale of medical science becomes a metaphor for performative *manning up* for the female in "Self-Experiment") and is a compelling anticipation of the plasticity and performativity of sex and gender identities in biomedical postmodernity. Interestingly, the female cyborg masquerading as a male in Wolf's story becomes a threat to the phallogocentric scientific imaginary precisely at the point when s/he posits a problem in the erotic economy by beginning to date the professor's daughter. It is at this point that Anders is instructed to return to his former female self. The entire episode exemplifies Andreas Huyssen's contention that "[a]s soon as the machine came to be perceived as a demonic, inexplicable threat and as harbinger of chaos and destruction . . . writers began to imagine the *Maschinenmensch* as woman" (70, italics in original).

In what could be read as a feminist response to Wolf's "Self-Experiment", Judith "Jack" Halberstam argues how the rise and increasing sophistication of cybernetics "simultaneously maps out the terrain for both postmodern discussions of the subject in late capitalism and feminist debates about technology, postmodernism and gender" (440). This takes place, as Halberstam argues, due to the blurring of borderlines between the mind and the body, organic and inorganic, human and non-human, as postmodern cybernetics levels away the binarism prevalent in Western metaphysics. In a comparative analysis of the Apple company logo (the half-bitten apple) and Donna Haraway's notion of the cyborg, Halberstam examines how the dominant iconography of the bitten apple (with *byte* replacing the *bite*) – exemplifying postmodern simulation – deconstructs and debunks the Biblical story of original sin through the scandalous proclamation that the "subject has always sinned, has never not bitten the apple" (440). This fits in perfectly with Haraway's reading of the cyborg as an originless organism with no knowledge of the Garden of Eden, the Creation narrative or the Oedipal libidinal economy. As Halberstam argues in her reading of the Apple logo, the female cyborg "replaces Eve in this myth with a figure who severs once and for all the assumed connection between woman and nature upon which entire patriarchal structures rest" (440).

Halberstam's article brings out the political and subversive quality of the indeterminacy directed against the politics of patriarchy, whereby the carefully controlled distinctions between male and female, natural and artificial, blur away. In a similar vein, in her analysis of the presence of the postmodern in feminist discourses, especially in relation to the legal parlance, American literary critic and Deconstructionist Barbara Johnson highlights the political quality underscoring indeterminacy. Defining gender as a fluid category and as a site to "begin the analysis again – a political imperative to go on" (1082), Johnson examines indeterminacy in identity as a political and epistemic condition. In her essay on the complex politics and varied perspectives in Anglo-American and French feminism, Toril Moi underlines the *intentional impossibility* in conservative feminism and offers an understanding of postfeminism that would be allied with the poetics of postmodernism. Such an alliance and the subsequent emergence of what she describes as postmodernist postfeminism may, in the words of Moi, offer a "uniquely enabling theoretical development which will permit us finally to escape the patriarchal paradigms of Western thought" (5). The postmodern notion of gender and generation of gender identities may be described, as Judith Butler does, as an embodied performance designed to achieve an affect and sometimes a spectacle. It thus resonates with the postmodern slipperiness between signifier and signified, between reality and virtuality, foregrounding the body as a site of play that unsettles shared notions about gender, biological behaviour and sexuality. It is interesting and yet unsurprising to note how many of the novels discussed in the previous chapter – including Will Self's *Dorian*, Thomas Pynchon's *Gravity's Rainbow* and William Gibson's *Neuromancer* – also offer complex readings of postmodernism, gender and performativity. The body in these novels is less a stable site with biological essence than a plastic performative play where the binaries between man and woman, human and machine, inorganic and organic, virtual and real, are permanently problematised.

Any study of postmodernism and gender must take into account the medical sciences of cosmetic surgery and sex change that became increasingly popular and accessible during the closing decades of the twentieth century and proliferated common consumer culture as well as the celebrity industry, as embodied by figures such as Michael Jackson and David Bowie (Constable 43–61). It corresponds to Jean Baudrillard's characterisation of postmodern consumer culture as an "orgy of liberation", where the liberated individual emerges as someone who "changes spaces, who circulates, who changes sex, clothes, and habits according to fashion, *rather than morality*" (96, italics in original). Baudrillard extends the examination of postmodern technocracy with a heightened attention to affect, resistance and identity, as examined in the previous chapter. There is thus a deep and complex correspondence between postmodernism and gender studies, with performativity being the connecting trope extending onto the domains of language, sexuality and the body. This is instantiated in the work of mid-twentieth-century French feminists such as Julia Kristeva, Hélène Cixous and Luce Irigaray, where the speaking subject is marked not by phallogocentric rationality and stability but instead by interruptions, contradictions and counter-narratives.

Even in their most generic forms, feminism and postmodernism both question the constructed qualities of gender and gendered identities as determined by Western male metaphysics of essence. In the process, both are marked by "researching gendered experience while simultaneously challenging the ontological status of both gender and experience" (Cosgrove 86).[3] As Judith Halberstam argues in her fascinating article on the interfaces between postmodernism and feminism, "[o]n the most basic level, feminism forces a theory of gender oppression upon postmodernism, and postmodernism provides feminism with a politics of artificiality" (447). This entanglement of organicity and artificiality subverts essentialised definitions and dualisms informing dominant gender norms. The connection between feminism and postmodernism is interestingly examined in the work of Barbara Creed who draws on the studies of Alice Jardine and Craig Owens to underline her investigation. Alluding specifically to Owens's work on this topic, Creed delineates the resonances and interfaces between feminism and postmodernism, especially as the two emerged in the latter half of the twentieth century. Creed describes the similarities thus:

> Both feminism and postmodernism endorse Lyotard's argument that there is a crisis in the legitimizing function of narrative, that the *grands récits* or Great Narratives of the West have lost credibility; both present a critique of representation . . . both present a critique of binarism, that is, thinking by means of

> oppositions; . . . both seek to heal the breach between theory and practice . . . both critique the privileging of vision as the superior sense and as the guarantor of truth. (48, italics in original)

Creed's description above is an illustration of the commonalities between feminism and postmodernism in terms of their interrogation of the grand narratives of patriarchy and phallogentricism. What emerges in both the movements is a resistance against and revision of the dominant definitions of gender, body and identity, as well as the advocation of a shift from the metaphysics of essence to an acceptance of "difference and incommensurability" (Owens 61–62). The postmodern subject, as Halberstam argues compellingly, "in its fragmentary and partial form, was formed out of the very challenge made by feminism to patriarchy" (449). In resonance with some of the key tenets of postmodernism, gender in the works of theorists such as Butler and Kristeva entails a "complex interplay between the psyche and performance, mediated by discourse and sustained by the desire-power-knowledge matrix" (Cosgrove 97) that questions the cultural and shared imaginary informing identity politics.

The work of Alice Jardine, especially her deployment of the term "gynesis" as a process of representation that requestions and rethinks hegemonic hierarchical notions about human identity, body and history, has been crucial for an understanding of the interface between postmodernism and gender studies. Drawing on the works of Derrida as well as Lacan, Jardine defines gynesis as "a reincorporation and reconceptualization of that which has been the master narrative's own 'non-knowledge', what has eluded them, what has engulfed them. This other-than-themselves is almost always a 'space' of some kind (over which the narrative has lost control), and this space has been coded as feminine, as woman" (25). With obvious allusions to Plato's notion of the *chora* – "an abyssal origin within which the very concept of the Beginning loses itself in its own proliferating doubles" (Margaroni 83) – Jardine's notion of gynesis is in resonance with Kristeva's definition of the *semiotic chora* and Irigaray's idea of the *two-lipped discourse* situated against productive patriarchy (patriarchal principles of production in a heteronormative capitalist matrix) and bears obvious extensions onto a study of postmodernity. In her 1974 work titled *Revolution in Poetic Language*, Kristeva draws on Plato's idea of the *chora* in *Timaeus* (c. 360BC) and describes it as a space for semiotic and epistemic fluidity with an entanglement of language and body.

In *Timaeus*, Plato defines the *chora* (*khôra*) as the third space that lies outside the mainstream territory of the metropolis. In Plato's philosophy, the *chora* is a space and a state between being and non-being and carries maternal metaphors of the matrix and the womb where meanings and identities are interrupted as well as re-formed. Drawing on Plato's dialogues in *Timaeus*, Jacques Derrida extends the notion of *khôra* as an

> . . . alternation between the logic of exclusion and that of participation . . . [which] stems perhaps only from a provisional appearance and from the constraints of rhetoric, even from some incapacity for naming . . . it 'participates' in the intelligible in a very troublesome and indeed aporetic way . . . it does not proceed from the natural or legitimate *logos* but rather from a hybrid, bastard, even corrupted reasoning (*logismonotho*). (89–90)

It is interesting to examine how Plato's *khôra* informs post-structuralist and feminist discourses on the aporia between the semiotic and symbolic orders of meaning and identity. As Maria Margaroni puts it, Kristeva draws on the Greek idea of *chora* (semeion) and defines it as a post-structuralist, feminist semiotic that emerges as a critique of post-Enlightenment logic by "signifying operation based on traces and marks rather than signs, the marks of the drives on the speaking body" (79). Kristeva's attempt in *Revolution in Poetic Language* is largely to highlight the corporeal amniotic quality of language that is effaced by production of meanings. It thus situates itself against the patriarchal principles informing the grand narratives of meaning and history and becomes a natural ally to the tenets of postmodernism.

In her Preface to *Desire in Language*, Kristeva defines the act of writing as a process of scription that "assumes the necessity of adopting a stance involving otherness, distance, even limitation" as the only ethical guarantee in a world overdetermined by technocratic rationality (ix). Elsewhere, drawing on Mikhail Bakhtin's notion of poetic language as a polyphonic construct, Kristeva describes how the subject of subversive language becomes its "own otherness, and thereby multiple and elusive, polyphonic" ("The Ruin of a Poetics" 109), opening up the play between the self and the signifier in the postmodernist politics of gender. Kristeva's distinction between the *géno-texte* and the *phéno-texte* is particularly crucial in the context of a postmodernist understanding of gender identities and their inscriptions. Her analysis here spills over onto the domain of postmodernist politics of writing as well. Thus, whereas the phenotext corresponds to a structure that "obeys rules of communication and presupposes a subject of enunciation and an addressee", the genotext corresponds not so much to a linguistic structure as to a "*process*, which tends to articulate structures that are ephemeral (unstable, threatened by drive charges, 'quanta' rather than 'marks') and nonsignifying (devices that do not have a double articulation)" ("Julia Kristeva in Conversation with Rosalind Coward" 26–27, italics in original). It is interesting to examine how Kristeva's notion of genotext applies to works of postmodernist literature such as Joyce's *Finnegans Wake* (1939) and Jeanette Winterson's *Written on the Body* (1992), a novel that will be examined subsequently in this chapter.

Perhaps the most powerful representation of the play between gender identities and the politics of deferred and slippery writing occurs in Kristeva's 1977 essay titled "Stabat Mater", which equates the politics of deferred writing – writing after – with the feminist enterprise to subvert the order of law by converting it into "flesh, language, *jouissance*" (262, italics in original) precisely through the act of giving the word flesh. The essay describes the grief of the mourning mother (Mary) before the corpse of her son (Jesus) and combines the cult of Mother Mary with Kristeva's personal accounts of her bodily and psychic experiences surrounding the birth of her son. The essay is a fine example of feminist writing that describes how "a new language and subjectivity may emerge that remains closer to the maternal body, its experiences and psychology" (Doane and Hodges 64). Kristeva achieves this in "Stabat Mater" by incorporating the semiotic *chora* into the body of the essay, investing an incestuous quality to the text through a process of contamination with primary narcissism (McCance 152). The act of *writing as bliss* corresponds to the post-structuralist subversion of standardised language as theorised by critics such as Roland Barthes. More significantly, from a more mainstream postmodernist perspective, this politics of deferred writing corresponds closely to Jean-François Lyotard's notion of the economy of deferral that characterises the self as "essentially passible to a recurrent alterity" in the cultural condition of postmodernity (59). Postmodernism, in Kristeva's feminist poetics, emerges as an attempt to "*expand the limits of the signifiable*" ("Postmodernism" 137, italics in original) and incorporates the aporia of the body as the site of inscription and subversion.

Like Kristeva's concept of the semiotic chora, Irigaray's description of the two-lipped discourse as an iconic representation of the woman appropriates the attitude of postmodernist poetics. Defining the symbol of the two lips as a discourse and a representation rather than a form of biological essentialism, Irigaray states,

> To seek to discover-rediscover a possible imaginary for women through the movement of two lips re-touching . . . does not mean

> a regressive recourse to anatomy or to a concept of 'nature', nor a recall to genital order – women have more than one pair of two lips! Rather it means to open up the autological and tautological circle of systems of representation and their discourse so that women may speak (of) their sex [*parler leur sexe*]. (*Parler n'est jamais neu* 272, italics in original)

In keeping with the postmodernist plurality and polyphony of signs and signifiers, Irigaray's iconography of the two lips extends as a metaphor for multiple identities inscribed as well as embodied. The other image that occurs in Irigaray's discursive representation of the body is that of the mucous, the state of slipperiness that is both subject and object, both solid and fluid, both inside and outside in terms of orders of embodiment. The mucous, for Irigaray, like the womb, inhabits the fluidity of embodiment and representation, one that is immediately incorporated in the order of inscription. Like Plato's *khôra* and Kristeva's feminist appropriation of the same, Irigaray's notion of the mucous represents the unrepresentable, the "[r]aw material, or a cast-off from what has already been born, it has yet to find its forms, to flower in accordance with its roots. It has still not been born into its own growth, its subjectivity" (*Sexes et parentés* 194). As Irigaray would describe it elsewhere, the symbol of the mucous is subversive inasmuch as it situates itself against the phallic economy of the controlled and contained body as well as against the rationale of Kant's transcendental aesthetic that is a complex of space and time informing the possibilities of experience. Instead, the irreverent interiority metaphorised by the mucous instantiates how "[t]he transition to a new age necessitates a new perception and a new conception of *time and space*, our *occupation of place*, and the *envelopes of identity*" (*Ethique de la différence sexuelle* 15, italics in original).

In keeping with the postmodernist poetics of performance and slippage, Alice Jardine's notion of gynesis offers an understanding of identity as text, one that can be unpacked and deconstructed. This is historicised by Jardine thus: "[t]he interrogative return to the sources of our knowledge in the West has involved an obligatory return to the mother's body – a female body, no matter how unrecognizable; no matter how hysterical, textual, inanimate, or actual" (237). In continuation of the postmodernist critique of the metaphysics of essence, the feminist critique enacted by Irigaray and Kristeva is directed against the phallogocentric principle that had historically informed Western Enlightenment logic. It is therefore interesting to examine the contemporaneity between radical feminism and postmodernism in terms of their historical growth and evolution. Thus, while Kristeva questions the very dichotomy of man/woman as belonging to the order of metaphysics, she also argues for the need to prioritise identification over identity as a means to interrogate such a humanist understanding of gender and sexuality. In a similar vein, Irigaray advocates a re-examination of gender as an endless horizon rather than a closure, a notion that bears interesting correspondence with Baudrillard's notion of the hyperreal that celebrates virtuality over and above ontological reality. The works of the French post-structuralist feminists such as Kristeva, Irigaray and Cixous offer a key to a nuanced understanding of the postmodern definition of gender. More importantly, these readings of gender as performativity spill over onto the domain of language in terms of the semiological and symbolic shifts they enact with an acute awareness of the gendered affect embedded in language. These aspects appear prominently and consistently in the works of Judith Butler.

In her 1999 preface to *Gender Trouble*, Butler draws attention to the fact that she drew on Derrida's reading of Kafka's short story "Before the Law" in order to produce the metaleptic and repetitive concept of *performativity*, thus revealing the literary legacy of the term where gender is embodied, extended and enacted through figurative as well as physical processes.

Drawing on the notion of the drag, Butler goes on to state the subversive component embedded in that definition:

> If one thinks that one sees a man dressed as a woman or a woman dressed as a man, then one takes the first term of each of those perceptions as the 'reality' of gender: the gender that is introduced through the simile lacks 'reality,' and is taken to constitute an illusory appearance. In such perceptions in which an ostensible reality is coupled with an unreality, we think we know what the reality is, and take the secondary appearance of gender to be mere artifice, play, falsehood, and illusion. (xxii)

It is interesting to examine the parallels between Butler's notion of the play between reality and artificiality and Baudrillard's notion of the simulacrum. Such parallels reveal how the ontic and embodied states in postmodernity are both marked by mutability and incommensurability rather than by narratives of stability and unity. More significantly, and in keeping with the tenets of posthumanism, Butler's notion of the drag combines reality with artificiality, organicity with inorganicity, playing up the interstices between embodiment and appearance through a "vacillation of categories" (xxiii).

The figure of the drag as examined by Butler is crucial for a nuanced understanding of gender and performance in postmodernity. Laying bare the fabricated unities that inform hegemonic heterosexuality, the drag enacts a corporeal radicalisation as well as a retelling of gender norms through a heightened attention to the polymorphous plurality of the body. The radicalisation enacted by the body of the drag is described thus by Butler:

> The performance of drag plays upon the distinction between the anatomy of the performer and the gender that is being performed. But we are actually in the presence of three contingent dimensions of significant corporeality: anatomical sex, gender identity, and gender performance. If the anatomy of the performer is already

> distinct from the gender of the performer, and both of these are distinct from the gender of the performance, then the performance suggests a dissonance not only between sex and performance, but sex and gender, and gender and performance. (175)

The drag thus opens up the divisions between anatomical identity and sexual identity through an embodied performance that constructs affective performativity. The notion of gender being performative and the extent to which this extends onto the domain of grammar of articulation is evinced in Butler's description of gender as "always a doing" (34), not a noun but a verb, a state that is endlessly produced and mutated by the body. By the same token, sex ceases to be a stable act for pleasure and procreation but a "performatively enacted signification" that can produce "parodic proliferation and subversive play of gendered meanings" (46).

Butler's work is an excellent examination of the interface between discursivity and corporeality that characterises postmodernity, advocating an alternate understanding of gender as performance. Her notion of performativity as the slippery enactment entangling the ontological and the figurative orders draws on the tenets of post-structuralism with its play between the signifier and the signified. Such politics of production and generation of identities are structurally as well as stylistically allied with the poetics of postmodernist writing, as evinced in the literary works that will be examined in this chapter. The term "performative" as employed by Butler suggests a "dramatic and contingent construction of meaning" (190) while offering a renewed understanding of language, affect and body. Butler concludes *Gender Trouble* by describing gender as a norm "that can never be fully internalized", a set of standards that "are finally phantasmatic, impossible to embody" (192).

It is important to examine the figure of the drag – as Butler does in her subsequent works – not as an easy and necessary subversion but as an *ambivalent act* that may or may not conform to the codes of hegemonic heterosexual behaviour. This is in consonance with the politics of indeterminacy highlighted by Barbara Johnson, as examined at the beginning of this chapter. In a more immediately postmodernist spirit, Butler's notion of ambivalence corresponds to the *irony of inconsistency* in postmodernist poetics whereby even inconsistency is not consistent and refuses to be radical ad infinitum. This is made evident in Butler's description in a later work where she warns against any simplistic reading of *Gender Trouble*:

> Although many readers understood *Gender Trouble* to be arguing for the proliferation of drag performances as a way of subverting dominant gender norms, I want to underscore that there is no necessary relation between drag and subversion, and that drag may well be used in the service of both the denaturalization and reidealization of hyperbolic heterosexual gender norms. At best, it seems, drag is a site of a certain ambivalence, one which reflects the more general situation of being implicated in the regimes of power by which one is constituted and, hence, of being implicated in the very regimes of power that one opposes. (*Bodies That Matter* 85)

As the site of ambivalence, the drag, like the mimic man in postcolonial theory (whose correspondences with postmodernism will be examined in the next chapter), is always an act of slippage, even from the point of view of subversion. It is thus not necessarily subversive but an ambivalent activity that requestions and reconfigures any ontology of origin. The theoretical alliances between postmodernism and Gender Studies inhabit the domains of discourse, technology and body, as exemplified by the cyborg and the drag. This is instantiated and dramatised in many major works of literature, as will be explored in the rest of this chapter.

Perhaps the writer who best exemplifies the interface between postmodernism and gender politics is Jeanette Winterson, whose novels examine what Catherine Belsey describes as the "extraordinary loquacity, a proliferation of textuality which calls into question the proprieties, complacencies and certainties of the past" (687) in postmodernist representations of love that interrogate any metaphysics of desire. Winterson's 1992 novel *Written on the Body* is a telling depiction of the drama of desire that describes the body as a play between fragmentation and wholeness, between remembered inscription and performative subversion, corroborating Judith Butler's claim that "[t]he construction of stable bodily contours relies upon fixed sites of corporeal permeability and impermeability" (*Gender Trouble* 132). Using an unreliable and unclear narrator with no name or gender and a narrative strategy designed to recreate an absent female body through evocative descriptions, Winterson in *Written on the Body* offers an excellent example of postmodernist feminist writing, one that plays with positional and sexual identities.

The play between desire and destruction is permanently problematised in *Written on the Body*, evinced thus in the narrator's ambivalent admission:

> What I wanted to do was to fasten my index finger and thumb at the bolts of your collar bone . . . . You asked me if I wanted to strangle you. No, I wanted to fit you, not just in the obvious ways but in so many indentations . . . . I thought difference was rated to be the largest part of sexual attraction but there are so many things about us that are the same. Bone of my bone. Flesh of my flesh. (129)

The passage reveals the promiscuous proximity between shared orders of difference and is a classic instantiation of postmodernist writing that plays with and problematises gender. The appropriation of the Biblical metaphors – "Bone of my bone. Flesh of my flesh" – also subverts the heteronormativity of divinely ordained desire by a deliberate deconstruction of the narrator's identity that swings between a butch guy and a lesbian lover. Winterson further flags up the postmodernist quality in her novel with intertextual allusions: "For her [Louise] pleasure was in . . . a game between equals who might not always choose to be equals. She was not a D. H. Lawrence type; no-one could take Louise with animal inevitability" (67). The fictionality and fluidity of gender identities are further corroborated in Winterson's novel as the narrator introspects, "What do I think I am? Sir Launcelot?" (159), dramatising a discursive play between chivalric masculinity and lesbian love while also generating what Heather Nunn describes as "post-genital erotic economy" (17) that is naturally allied with postmodernist poetics of representation.

Written on the Body exemplifies the postmodernist strategy of entanglement at the level of representation whereby metaphors from different and disparate fields of enquiry are enmeshed in order to describe difference and sameness. This is evinced by the virtual narrator's statement of romantic fusion: "There are many ways to fit molecules together but only a few juxtapositions that bring them close enough to bond. . . . We touch one another, bond and break, drift away on force-fields we don't understand" (61–62). This description of love at the level of molecules not only draws attention to the biological materialism of the body but also breaks away and spills onto the domain of indeterminacy at the level of embodiment and identity. This play between fracture and fusion takes place at the level of the self–other relationship in Winterson's novel as well as at the metacognitive level of psychological situatedness whereby the narrator looks at her/his reflection in the mirror and confesses, "It's not my own face I see. Your body is twice. Once you once me. Can I be sure which is which?" (99) The confusion at the level of cognition and embodiment underscores the broader narrative of gender indeterminacy in Winterson's novel that incorporates a postmodernist strategy of representation which dramatises the "shock of nonrecognition" (LaBelle 100).

At a fundamental level, Winterson's *Written on the Body* exemplifies the postmodernist play between self and story, between neurons and narratives, evinced immediately in the narrator's address to her/his beloved Louise's bodily scars: "There's a story trapped inside your mouth. A crashed car and a smashed windscreen" (117). A classic instantiation of the play between textuality and embodied identity, Winterson's novel describes lovemaking as an act of reading as well as an act of discovery – the narrator uses the metaphor of Columbus sighting the Americas in order to describe her/his erotic experiences with Louise – while also describing how the latter has "translated me into her own book" (89). The cartographic quality of the erotic body and the ambivalent act of lovemaking – it is never clear in Winterson's novel whether the narrator and Louise share a heterosexual or homosexual love – is further highlighted in the novel by the following statement made by the narrator: "I will explore you and mine you and you will redraw me according to your will. We shall cross one another's boundaries and make ourselves one nation" (20). In a complex of plasticity and performativity, love and gender in Winterson's novel emerge as mutable activities rather than stable identities, with the metaphor of the nation highlighting the organic as well as the constructed qualities of desire.

In a fascinating article entitled "Winterson, Bakhtin and the Chronotope of a Lesbian Hero", Mary Bratton argues how Winterson's 1989 novel *Sexing the Cherry* appropriates the Bakhtinian notion of the chronotope – the complex/continuum of fluid space and time – in order to problematise the location of lesbian heroes in their movements across time. Winterson does this explicitly in *Sexing the Cherry* by a strategic and stylistic superimposition of narrative time and carnival time that emerges as an interface and interplay between historical and psychological situatedness. This is described by Bratton in her article:

> Winterson's texts reveal their tensions of time/space and the lesbian/female hero by holding out on connecting their

> chronotopes with either of these forms of time in a gendered binary (and this resistance is the condition for a lesbian chronotope in her texts). For example, the narration of *Written on the Body* occurs mostly in linear time, but the lack of gender labeling for the narrator subverts the biographical development of the plot because a reader becomes aware that something that is routinely part of linear development is missing. (212)

The passage above reveals the postmodern gender politics in Winterson's novels that is further problematised by a play of different orders of time, a rich and complex category of representation whereby gender indeterminacy and temporal indeterminacy are entangled together.

A profoundly postmodernist text that plays with historical and gendered identities, Winterson's *Sexing the Cherry* contains narrative switches between a seventeenth–century male named Jordan and "Dog-Woman", and twentieth–century Nicolas Jordan and an unnamed woman. The grotesque seventeenth–century "Dog-Woman" and the mid-twentieth–century madwoman are both unnamed in Winterson's novel, whereas the men are mediated and identified through history and historical events. Jordon in *Sexing the Cherry* uses the figure of his beloved Fortunata as a signifier of absence against which his physical presence is marked: "I begin to row, using her body as a marker. I always will" (103). The complex relationship shared by the Dog-Woman and Fortunata in *Sexing the Cherry* emerges as a counter-narrative to the patriarchal paradigms of power. Thus, whenever the Dog-Woman sees Fortunata standing next to Jordon, the narrative informs readers that he cannot see her at that point. Although Fortunata is figuratively linked to all the women in Winterson's novel across different points in historical time, her narrative does not inhabit the carnivalesque quality characterising the stories of other women, situating her in a complex yet unreal relationship with the men who inhabit historical time in *Sexing the Cherry*.

As Bratton argues in her article, Winterson's *Sexing the Cherry* superimposes two different orders of chronotope – the historical and the carnivalesque – in relation to the ways gender roles are played out in the narrative, thus making the novel a fascinating work in postmodernist poetics that dramatises performativity in historical as well as gender identities. In her article on *Sexing the Cherry* entitled "Sexing the Text", Elizabeth Langland examines how the Dog-Woman in Winterson's novel functions in a manner similar to that of the drag as theorised by Judith Butler. Thus, the Dog-Woman is attributed an order of activity that "decrees a different social performance and reception of those normative expressions and disrupts the would-be unity among anatomical sex, gender identity and gender performance" (Langland 103). The complex gender attributes of the Dog-Woman in Winterson's novel are interestingly and ironically voiced through her son Jordon whose description assumes an aspirational quality at the level of heroic identity: "I want to be like my rip-roaring mother who cares nothing for how she looks, only for what she does. She has never been in love, no, and never wanted to be either. She is self-sufficient and without self doubt. . . . She is silent, the way men are supposed to be" (114). This description of a carnivalesque woman from a male who aspires to model himself on the masculine tenets of British imperialism invests a contingency and complexity in the economy of gender identifications in Winterson's novel, whose very title evokes a performative play of sexual identities.

The politics of masculinity and masculine identifications in Winterson's postmodern novel is further dramatised with the seventeenth–century Jordan's more contemporary counterpart Nicolas, as the narrative cuts across time and moves into the twentieth century. A consumer of *The Boy's Handbook*, Nicolas has less masculine anxiety than Jordan and readily identifies his male heroes: William the Conqueror, Christopher Columbus, Francis Drake and Lord Nelson, an assortment of imperialists, voyagers and military men who embody historically hegemonic masculine orders. The recipe of heroism rattled off by the young Nicolas – constructed out of textbook accounts of male chivalry – is predictably normative:

> If you're a hero you can be an idiot, behave badly, ruin your personal life, have any number of mistresses and talk about yourself all the time, and nobody minds. Heroes are immune. They have wide shoulders and plenty of hair and wherever they go a crowd gathers. Mostly they enjoy the company of other men, although attractive women are part of their reward. (132)

The unquestioning consumption of hegemonic heroism and the classification of women as attractive rewards emerges as a subtle critique of the same in Winterson's novel which ascribes true heroism to the loveless and fearless Dog-Woman who fights to liberate London from religious hypocrisy, an account that is understandably absent in narratives of history and which Nicolas comes to know of through conversations with his friend Jack.

Moving away from his earlier masculinist model of heroism, Nicolas confesses that true heroism lies not in biological attributes of manliness but in giving up "what's comfortable in order to protect what they believe in or to live dangerously for the common good" (158–59), a realisation that is accompanied by his enquiry about the misogynistic treatment meted out to the Dog-Woman in the seventeenth century, despite her true bravery and sacrifices for a heroic cause. The epigraph of Winterson's *Sexing the Cherry* combines the complexity of gender and embodied identities with a voice of scepticism that is typically postmodernist in its philosophical and scientific introspection on the ontology of matter: "[m]atter, that thing the most solid and the well-known, which you are holding in your hands and which makes up your body, is now known to be mostly empty space. Empty space and points of light. What does this say about the reality of the world?" (8) Winterson's novel, with its play between identities and non-identities, across historical and carnivalesque orders of time, is also a play between matter and its absence, dramatising the fact that the two orders are not necessarily oppositional but ontologically interdependent, like memory and forgetting.

With a typically postmodernist strategy of indeterminacy whereby the characters unlearn their privilege and reach out for less stable, more contingent narratives of identity and identification, Winterson's *Sexing the Cherry* has the seventeenth-century male Jordan state:

> I have set off and found that there is no end to even the simplest journey of the mind. I begin, and straight away a hundred alternative routes present themselves.... Every time I try to narrow down my intent I expand it, and yet those straits and canals still lead me to the open sea, and then I realize how vast it all is, this matter of the mind. (115)

The hundred alternative routes may be read as metaphors of epistemological pathways in the curious mind of Jordan who inhabits the cusp of emerging British imperialism. But it may also be read in resonance with the postmodern plurality in Winterson's novel whereby characters emerge as a play between presence and non-presence. This is immediately corroborated in Jordon's confession of his desire for Fortunata when he expresses his confusion as to whether he is "searching for a dancer ... or for the dancing part of myself" (39). The metonymic quality of association and identification in Winterson's novel is an instantiation of its postmodernist quality, one that invests itself into a renewed and radical examination of gender roles and identities. *Sexing the Cherry* achieves this "in its affiliation with the postmodern novel and in its performance of that postmodernity [whereby] it constantly challenges the linearity of argument and the possibility of progression implicit in an ability to pose issues in a hierarchical and dialectical way" (Langland 106). Winterson's novel displays a postmodernist intertextual strategy whereby it alludes to the seventeenth-century poem "The Mower, Against Gardens" (1681) by Andrew Marvell while also subverting the stability Marvell's lyric aspires to achieve through its pastoral and idyllic imagery. Through an appropriation of the drag performance, as Langland argues, Winterson's *Sexing the Cherry* destabilises the dualisms of self and other, man and woman, and past and present, with its postmodernist poetics allied to a feminist politics "wherein the mutual complicity of these categories is read not simply as a deconstruction but as the basis for a feminist praxis that avoids the exclusionary normativity of proceeding from an assumed coherence of the category woman" (106).

The deconstruction of the category of the woman is powerfully dramatised in Joanna Russ's 1975 work *The Female Man*. Like Winterson's *Sexing the Cherry*, Russ in her novel invests invisibility to the woman who inhabits a world that constantly questions the limitations and constructed qualities of common sense. This is examined by Donna Haraway, especially in relation to her own work:

> This book [*The Female Man*] made gender a patent scandal of the imagination, the intellect, nature, language, and history – all those hoary categories in the romances of modernity . . . The linguistic and genetic miscegenation of both Russ's Female Man and my FemaleMan© is a tool for provoking a little technical and political intercourse, or criminal conversation, or reproductive commerce, about what counts as nature, for whom, and at what cost. (75)

Haraway's description of Russ's novel is a critical, theoretical corroboration of the polymorphous plurality around gender roles and identity allied to the deconstructive poetics of postmodernism. Like Winterson's *Sexing the Cherry*, Russ's novel charts the journeys of different human figures across different points in historical time, through a process of dislocation and entanglement. The discourse of dualism determining gender relations in the normative world is evocatively articulated by the character Joanna in Russ's novel, who declares herself as a "Female Man". Joanna attributes her agony to "the knowledge you suffer when you're an outsider. . . . That knowledge is, of course, the perception of all experience through two sets of eyes, two systems of value, two habits of expectation, almost two minds" (137–38). *The Female Man* is a postmodernist novel that seeks to subvert the binary quality of gendered mappings and their consequent embodied existences.

There are four females in Russ's novel – the librarian Jeannine Nancy Dadier who inhabits a world still enmeshed in the Great Depression, who initially conforms to the regenerative possibility of marriage but ends up being broken and participating in a social revolution against patriarchy, the "female man" Joanna who happens to inhabit a place similar to the Earth, the Safety and Peace Officer Janet Evason Belin who hails from the futuristic world called Whileaway where all men died 800 years ago in a plague affecting just the males. Janet is married to Vittoria, has two children and is absolutely unaware of the perils of male control, having never experienced male domination in an all-women world. The fourth J in Russ's novel is Alice-Jael Reasoner, referred to as Jael, an assassin in a world marked by a gender war for forty years. Seemingly unemotional and steadfastly radical, Jael is instrumental in arranging a meeting of the four women in Russ's novel in order to execute a revolution against men across the world. Through a complex interplay across these four female figures, Russ's novel emerges as feminist science fiction as well as a female *bildungsroman*, one whose scandal, as Jennifer Wagner-Lawlor argues, lies in its "blustering insistence that both men and women *see* the nature of ideological unknowing, and admit to the self-interestedness in dwelling among the community of 'partial knowers' who are too afraid or too stubborn to learn" (17, italics in original).

Technology in Russ's novel – most dramatically depicted in the futuristic world of Whileaway – emerges as a necessary apparatus in an all-woman space where male control and presence have been clinically killed. Depicting a world of genetic engineering through parthenogenesis that effaces all male intervention at existential as well as biological levels, the women in Whileaway do not view technology as either help or hindrance but as an almost passive presence that has been entirely internalised. A similar view of technology occurs in the gender-warring space inhabited by Jael where machines simply stay in order to be appropriated and executed. The presence of technology here is dramatised in the figure of Davy, a robot designed as an attractive male intended to offer sexual pleasure to Jael, as her cyborg boyfriend, in a curious reversal of reification at the level of dominant gender roles in a world where, as Donna Haraway writes, "miscegenation between and among humans and nonhumans is the norm" (121). Technology in Russ's novel, as Susana S. Martins argues, offers a "way of talking about temporality and change, about historicity and futurity, including agential social change" (406). With its entanglement of human and machine, female and male, Russ's *The Female Man* is an excellent example of postmodernist science fiction that radically engages with issues of gender and gendered identities in complex chronotopes that cut into and across each other. This is evinced by the structure of the novel that is divided into nine parts with sub-chapters that further cut into each other, blending politics as well as points of view in a heteroglossic imagination.

There are strategic movements of time and space, as demonstrated in part five of the novel that begins in Jeannine's world but quickly cuts into Joanna's point of view. The experimentation with points of view is demonstrated also in Joanna, Janet and Jael's stories that are mostly narrated in first person with quick cuts into third person accounts. The fluidity of perspectives in Russ's novel is equated with the fluidity of female ...poreality, with the artist Joanna stating: "I have no structure

. . . my thoughts seep out shapelessly like menstrual fluid, it is all very female and deep and full of essences, it is very primitive and full of 'and's,' it is called 'run-on-sentences'" (137), in an appropriation of what the French feminists described as *écriture féminine*, the fluid female language that is best represented through acts of embodiment. The stylistic subversions in Russ's *The Female Man* extend onto a deconstruction of normative gender narratives, questioning "cultural contradictions and apparent binaries by creating borderline figures, hybrids, in a kind of dialectics that confounds categorical distinctions often assumed to be natural" (Martins 407). The questioning of gendered presuppositions takes place most radically in Russ's novel through the figure of Janet, the visitor from the all-female utopia, who is amused as well as appalled at the constructed and nefarious nature of normalcy in the world men and women ordinarily inhabit. In the process the novel awakens the readers, as all postmodernist works do, to the *unnaturalness of the natural world*.

This chapter has attempted to investigate the interfaces between postmodernism and gender studies inasmuch as both question the constructed qualities informing the politics of identity and identity formation. The discourses of feminism, especially French feminism as exemplified in the works of Irigaray, Cixous and Kristeva, find direct resonances and parallels with the discourses of the postmodernist avant-garde as examined by theorists such as Gayatri Spivak[4]. Spiritually and stylistically allied to "stylized repetition of acts" (Butler, *Gender Trouble* 140) that often eschew any ontology of origin, both postmodernism and Gender Studies are rooted in their attack against the metaphysics of essence that informs the grand narratives of production and patriarchy. Against such narratives, the postmodernist texts that problematise gender identities situate mutable plastic selves created through a complex of fantasy and desire (Palmer 111). What is achieved in the process is an entanglement of parody and performativity that becomes immediately political in its scope inasmuch as it is directed against essentialised entities and identities that are revealed as "fictional, nonrepresentational activity" (Flax 38).

The chapter began with a reference to a Christa Wolf story and will conclude with a reference to another Wolf narrative in order to further examine the interface between postmodernism and feminism. In her reading of Wolf's 1976 novel *Patterns of Childhood*, Linda Hutcheon investigates how remembering and forgetting form a crucial part of continuity at an existential level in a totalitarian regime. In alliance with the examination in the chapter on postmodernism, history and memory in this book, Hutcheon argues how Wolf's novel about the landscape of lost childhood and its nostalgia set in Nazi Landsberg emerges as an "example of the second kind of feminist-inspired postmodern writing about the self and its relation to time and place" (Hutcheon, *The Politics of Postmodernism* 163). Incorporating the metafictional self-referential quality that commonly characterises postmodernist poetics – Wolf's novel contains passages such as "[f]rom the beginning this chapter had been earmarked to deal with the war; like all the other chapters, it has been prepared on sheets with headings such as Past, Present, Trip to Poland, Manuscript" (164) – *Patterns of Childhood* offers an excellent example of feminist writing that allies itself with the stylistic politics of postmodernism with its bewildering description of total amnesia about wars and its admission that "it's so much easier . . . to invent the past than to remember it" (153).

As Linda Hutcheon argues in her analysis of Wolf's *Patterns of Childhood* as a feminist postmodernist text, postmodernism and feminism can inform each other at interesting interfaces where affect and agency intersect. Thus, Hutcheon states,

> [t]here is, then, a two-way involvement of the postmodern with the feminist: on the one hand, feminisms have successfully urged postmodernism to reconsider – in terms of gender – its challenges to that humanist universal called 'Man' and have supported and reinforced its de-naturalization of the separation between the private and the public, the personal and the political; on the other hand, postmodern parodic representational strategies have offered feminist artists an effective way of working within and yet challenging dominant patriarchal discourses. (*The Politics of Postmodernism* 167)

Crucially, in the alliance of postmodernism and Gender Studies, the site of subversion is most often the body and the deconstruction often emerges as enacted, extended and embodied in the way it blurs the borders between organic and inorganic, natural and artificial, and female and male, as evinced in the literary works examined in this chapter. Appropriating the aesthetic of irony and indeterminacy, postmodernist representations of gender and gendered identities are playful, irreverent and often deliberately unreal and incomplete, celebrating scandal and dramatising shock. Perhaps more than any other genre of writing, postmodernist subversions of gender and gendered performance exemplify Linda Hutcheon's notion of *irony's edge*: "not as saying one thing and meaning another . . . but instead as a process of communication that entails two or more meanings being played off, one against the other. . . . It plays between meanings, in a space that is always affectively charged, that always has a critical edge" (*Irony's Edge* 105). The affective quality of irony is dramatised and performed in the literary texts examined above as well as in the works of theorists who have been discussed. The most recurrent trait in postmodernist representations of gender and embodiment, however, is their deconstruction of dualism and continuous explorations of alternative spaces of affective articulation.

This naturally extends onto a critique of heteronormativity and the binary of sexual identities. In doing so, postmodernist representations of gender and gender identities corroborate the reality that "[a]ll understanding is interpretative and depends upon and must be expressed in and through preexisting contexts or language games" (Flax 39). The theories and representations of the gender problematic in postmodernist poetics reveal that gender – like history, culture, language and identity – is less an essence and more a text, and like all texts, is informed by construction and consolidation. The knowledge of textuality is the first step towards the possibility of deconstruction, one that offers an alternative "engagement with the here and now, [as well as] . . . the desire for something else, for something 'elsewhere'" (Lefanu 53).

Works Cited

Baudrillard, Jean. *Simulations.* Trans. Paul Foss, Paul Patton and Philip Beitchman. New York: Semiotext, 1983. Print.

Belsey, Catherine. "Postmodern Love: Questioning the Metaphysics of Desire." *New Literary History* 25.3 (1994): 683–705. Print.

Bratton, Mary. "Winterson, Bakhtin, and the Chronotope of a Lesbian Hero." *Journal of Narrative Theory* 32.2 (2002): 207–26. Print.

Butler, Judith. *Bodies That Matter: On the Discursive Limits of "Sex".* London & New York: Routledge, 1993. Print.

---. *Gender Trouble: Feminism and the Subversion of Identity.* New York: Routledge, 1999. Print.

Constable, Catherine. "Postmodernism and Film." *The Cambridge Companion to Postmodernism.* Ed. Steven Connor. Cambridge: Cambridge UP, 2004. 43–61. Print.

Cosgrove, Lisa. "Feminism, Postmodernism, and Psychological Research." *Hypatia* 18.3 (2003): 85–112. Print.

Creed, Barbara. "From Here to Modernity: Feminism and Postmodernism." *Screen* 28.2 (1987): 47–67. Print.

Derrida, Jacques. *On the Name*. Ed. Thomas Dutoit. Trans. David Wood, John P. Leavey Jr. and Ian McLeod. Stanford: Stanford UP, 1995. Print.

Doane, Janice, and Devon Hodges. *From Klein to Kristeva: Psychoanalytic Feminism and the Search for the "Good Enough" Mother*. Ann Arbor: U of Michigan P, 1992. Print.

Eigler, Friederike. "Rereading Christa Wolf's 'Selbstversuch': Cyborgs and Feminist Critiques of Scientific Discourse." *The German Quarterly* 73.4 (Autumn 2000): 401–15. Print.

Flax, Jane. *Thinking Fragments: Psychoanalysis, Feminism, and Postmodernism in the Contemporary West*. Berkeley: U of California P, 1990. Print.

Halberstam, Judith. "Automating Gender: Postmodern Feminism in the Age of the Intelligent Machine." *Feminist Studies* 17.3 (1991): 439–60. Print.

Haraway, Donna. *Modest_Witness@Second_Millennium. FemaleMan© _Meets_OncoMouse*™. New York: Routledge, 1997. Print.

Hermann, Anne. "The Transsexual as Anders in Christa Wolf's 'Self-Experiment'." *Genders* 3 (1988): 43–56. Print.

Hutcheon, Linda. *Irony's Edge: The Theory and Politics of Irony*. New York: Routledge, 1995. Print.

---. *The Politics of Postmodernism*. London: Routledge, 1989. Print.

Huyssen, Andreas. "The Vamp and the Machine: Fritz Lang's *Metropolis*." *After the Great Divide: Modernism, Mass Culture, Postmodernism*. Bloomington and Indianapolis: Indiana UP, 1986. Print.

Irigaray, Luce. *Ethique de la différence sexuelle*. Trans. Margaret Whitford. Paris: Minuit, 1984. Print.

---. *Parler n'est jamais neu*. Trans. Margaret Whitford. Paris: Minuit, 1985. Print.

---. *Sexes et parentés*. Trans. Margaret Whitford. Paris: Minuit, 1987. Print.

Jardine, Alice. *Gynesis, Configurations of Woman and Modernity*. Ithaca and London: Cornell UP, 1985. Print.

Johnson, Barbara. "The Postmodern in Feminism." *Harvard Law Review* 105.5 (March, 1992): 1076–83. Print.

Kristeva, Julia. *Desire in Language: A Semiotic Approach to Literature and Art*. Ed. Leon Roudiez. Trans. Thomas Gora, Alice Jardine and Leon Roudiez. New York: Columbia UP, 1980. Print.

---. "Julia Kristeva in Conversation with Rosalind Coward." *Desire*. Ed. Lisa Appignanesi. London: ICA Documents, 1984. 22–27. Print.

---. "Postmodernism?" *Romanticism, Modernism, Postmodernism*. Ed. Harry. R. Garvin. Lewisberg, PA: Buchnell UP, 1980. 136–41. Print.

---. "Stabat Mater." *Tales of Love*. Trans. Leon Roudiez. New York: Columbia UP, 1987. 234–64. Print.

---. "The Ruin of a Poetics." *Russian Formalism*. Ed. Stephen Bann and John E. Bowlt. Edinburgh: Scottish Academic P, 1973. 102–19. Print.

LaBelle, Jeninoy. *Herself Beheld: The Literature of the Looking Glass*. Ithaca: Cornell UP, 1988. Print.

Langland, Elizabeth. "Sexing the Text: Narrative Drag as Feminist Poetics and Politics in Jeanette Winterson's *Sexing the Cherry*." *Narrative* 5.1 (1997): 99–107. Print.

Lefanu, Sarah. *Feminism and Science Fiction*. Bloomington, IN: Indiana UP, 1989. Print.

Lyotard, Jean-François. *The Inhuman: Reflections on Time*. Trans. Geoffrey Bennington and Rachel Bowlby. Stanford: Stanford UP, 1991. Print.

Margaroni, Maria. "'The Lost Foundation': Kristeva's Semiotic *Chora* and its Ambiguous Legacy." *Hypatia* 20.1 (2005): 78–98. Print.

Martins, Susana S. "Revising the Future in 'The Female Man'." *Science Fiction Studies* 32.3 (2005): 405–22. Print.

McCance, Dawne. "L'écriture limite: Kristeva's Postmodern Feminist Ethics." *Hypatia* 11.2 (1996): 141–60. Print.

Moi, Toril. "Feminism, Postmodernism, and Style: Recent Feminist Criticism in the United States." *Cultural Critique* 9 (1988): 3–22. Print.

Nunn, Heather. "*Written on the Body*: An Anatomy of Horror, Melancholy and Love." *Women: A Cultural Review* 7.1 (1996): 16–27. Print.

Owens, Craig. "The Discourse of Others: Feminists and Postmodernism." *The Anti-Aesthetic: Essays on Postmodern Culture*. Ed. Hal Foster. Port Townsend: Bay Press, 1983. 57–82. Print.

Palmer, Paulina. "*The Passion*: Storytelling, Fantasy, Desire." *"I'm telling you stories": Jeanette Winterson and the Politics of Reading*. Ed. Helena Grice and Tim Woods. Amsterdam and Atlanta: Rodopi, 1998. 103–16. Print.

Russ, Joanna. *The Female Man*. New York: Bantam Books, 1975. Print.

Wagner-Lawlor, Jennifer A. *Postmodern Utopias and Feminist Fictions*. Cambridge: Cambridge UP, 2013. Print.

Winterson, Jeanette. *Sexing the Cherry*. London: Vintage, 2001. Print.

---. *Written on the Body*. London: Vintage, 1993. Print.

Wolf, Christa. *Patterns of Childhood*. Trans. Ursule Molinaro and Hedwig Rappolt. New York: Farrar, Straus and Giroux, 1980. Print.

---. "Self-Experiment: Treatise on a Report." *What Remains and Other Stories*. Trans. Heike Schwarzbauer and Rick Takvorian. New York: Farrar, Strauss and Giroux, 1993. 197–230. Print.

Notes

1. In her examination of Wolf's story, Hermann reads the experiment as more of a textual change than a sexual change, thus dramatising the entanglement of textuality and sexuality in postmodern notions of gender, their inscriptions and orders of embodiment.

2. In her interesting analysis of Wolf's story as a critique of phallogocentric scientific understanding, Eigler examines how the identity of the woman trying to balance private life with the professional demands in the scientific field is derogatively described as a "falsely programmed cybernetic mouse" (404) while

the story itself emerges as a commentary on the combination of scientific and authorial identities characterising the female protagonist in a postmodern culture, an early response to "Haraway's call for women's involvement in technology and the sciences" (411).

3. In her excellent analysis of the entanglement between feminist study and postmodernism, Cosgrove examines how Judith Butler's notion of performativity and Julia Kristeva's study of gender as positionality offer potentials of critique and subversion within closed studies of gender identities.
4. Spivak examines these commonalities in her article entitled "French Feminism in an International Frame".

FOUR

Postmodernism and the Postcolonial

At the beginning of Salman Rushdie's *Shame* (1983), the narrator – who sets out to tell stories by inventing what never happened to him – is interrupted by a voice that challenges the former's authority to articulate on his chosen subject:

> *Outsider! Trespasser! You have no right to this subject!* . . . I know: nobody ever arrested me. Nor are they ever likely to. *Poacher! Pirate! We reject your authority. We know you, with your foreign language wrapped around you like a flag: speaking about us in your forked tongue, what can you tell but lies?* I reply with more questions: is history to be considered the property of the participants solely? In what courts are such claims staked, what boundary commissions map out the territories? Can only the dead speak? (19, italics in original)

A novel about migration, nationality and identity in an increasingly globalising world, *Shame* may be regarded as a literary text that investigates the interface between the postmodern and postcolonial orders of existence with its dramatisation of ethnic and linguistic pluralities. Connected to this are the issues of agency and articulation apropos of history in postcolonial landscapes where right and rejection (as stated in the passage above) emerge less as calibrated categories than as *acts of appropriation* that may be simultaneously subversive and authoritative. In the process, *Shame* – a retelling of the life of Omar Khayyam set in the fictional town of "Q." and an allegory of the 1947 India–Pakistan Partition – dramatises "the question of vision and imagination in ways more complicated than a straightforward identification of the realist or the factual with the political might suggest" (Chakrabarty 150).

Through its imaginative historicisation and emplotment of historical narratives, *Shame*, like *The Moor's Last Sigh* (1995), dramatises the subversion of the Enlightenment notion of historical consciousness by "open-ended concepts of the past" whereby myths and legends define cultural identities (Nandy 44). This is achieved through ironic inversions and micro-narratives of magic and experientiality that interrogate as well as inform shared notions of history and historical identities. This incorporates an entanglement of postmodern politics of irony and postcolonial production of hyphenated signifiers addressed against the grand narratives of historical and cultural identities while stating how "[t]ime cannot be homogenized as easily as milk" (Rushdie 4). Rushdie achieves this through a narrator who rejoices in his ambivalent location in relation to the culture he describes, even as he confesses that he is a "translated man" who has been "borne across" while also stating how something is lost as well as gained in translation (Rushdie 29). Like *Shame*, and emerging as a novel that "deliberately and self-consciously assumes as intertexts a massive range of Eastern and Western cultural references that extends from Aeschylus to Isaac Asimov, the Mahabharata to Madonna, the Rig-Veda to Bollywood films" (Warnes 97), Rushdie's *Satanic Verses* (1988) acts as an excellent example of postmodern pastiche that is also a postcolonial retelling of the grand narratives of ethnographic and metaphysical identities. This chapter will examine such entanglement through a study of selected texts and critical strategies.

In his 1991 essay titled "Is the Post- in Postmodernism the Post- in Postcolonial?" Kwame Anthony Appiah argues that the dominant attitudes in the two isms are largely and mutually irreconcilable, with the postcolonial writer or intellectual in the non-white world overdetermined intellectually and economically by the critical tools and publishing politics of the Western world. Thus, Appiah states, the post-realism of a writer like Yambo Ouologuem is distinctly different from the post-realism of Thomas Pynchon (349). Although largely influential and true to much of the general condition of literary production from the "Third World" and its associated politics, Appiah's essay – which starts with a study of African art objects in the Centre for African Art in New York in 1987 – perhaps misses some of the salient similarities between the two isms in terms of their objectives and politics of representation. Even in their most fundamental ontological states, postmodernism and postcolonialism are essentially allied in their interrogations of the hegemonic discourses informing cultural, gender and racial identities, with qualities such as "the decentring of discourse, the focus on the significance of language and writing in the construction of experience, the use of the subversive strategies of mimicry, parody and irony", consistently creating a "conflation of the two fields" (Ashcroft 13).

One of the most fertile fields to investigate this conflation, one which is pregnant with histories of appropriations and subversions, is South Asian Literature in English, which, as Peter Morey argues, contains works that "often inscribe an implicit dialogue or creative tension between the overt political programme of postcolonialism and the linguistic focus of postmodernism" (82–83). It is this entanglement of political condition and linguistic subversion that characterises the postmodern postcolonial, which perhaps finds one of its earliest literary examples in Salman Rushdie's *Midnight's Children* (1981). Among the categories of representation that emblematise this political and linguistic entanglement are *hybridity* and *mimicry*, terms that crucially connect postmodernism as well as postcolonial studies. Both terms corroborate – in their discursive disseminations as well as stylised representations – Bakhtin's notion of language as a "two-sided act", one which "lies on the borderline between oneself and the other" (293). Both dramatise representations of asymmetrical heterogeneity and simultaneity, breaking away as well as directed against dominant discourses on language, location and identity.

Made famous in the works of Homi Bhabha, hybridity and mimicry underline the interstitial and liminal qualities of identity formation in political contact zones marked as well as mapped by cultural and epistemic exchanges. Essentially allied to the postmodernist politics of pastiche, mimicry in postcolonial studies entails a play between identity and its subversion, between presence and its problematic production. According to Bhabha's theorisation in his postcolonial discourse, mimicry is the slippage between appropriation and misappropriation, an ambivalent act whereby the native approximates as well as exceeds the original ontology of the coloniser through a performative process that attitudinally allies itself with the notion of performativity in gender studies, as examined in the previous chapter. As a play of identities, mimicry emerges as the site as well as the spectacle for subversion, producing in its wake a structure of sly civility whereby "[b]etween the civil address and its colonial signification – each axis displaying a problem of recognition and repetition – shuttles the signifier of authority in search of a strategy of surveillance, subjection, and inscription". This generates a liminality and an ambivalent affect of association/identification whereby "[b]oth colonizer and colonized are in a process of miscognition where each point of identification is always a partial and double repetition" (*The Location of Culture* 138–39). The threat that is enacted through hypercivility is further accentuated through language for Bhabha, as mimicry in the colonial space emerges as a subversive act of spectacular resistance. Thus, for Bhabha, "[w]hen the words of the master become the site of hybridity . . .

then we may not only read between the lines, but even seek to change the often coercive reality that they so lucidly contain" ("Signs Taken for Wonders" 162).

The ambivalence theorised by Bhabha in his description of postcolonial mimicry whereby "in order to be effective, mimicry must continually produce its slippage, its excess, its difference" ("Of Mimicry and Man" 126), corresponds complexly to Linda Hutcheon's description of the postmodernist parody which emerges as an "exploration of difference and similarity" whereby the "text may self-consciously present its own creative processes, perhaps as a model of man's exercise of language and meaning production" (25). As a complex of production and performativity, subversion and mimesis, mimicry as described in postcolonial studies resonates richly with the "patchwork of quotations and ironic paraphrases" (Hoesterey 95) that informs the postmodernist pastiche. The postmodern postcolonial thus emerges as an aesthetic that aims to generate as well as celebrate hybridity that is defined in postcolonial studies as

> . . . the revaluation of the assumption of colonial identity through the repetition of discriminatory identity effects. It displays the necessary deformation and displacement of all sites of discrimination and domination. It unsettles the mimetic and narcissistic demands of colonial power but reimplicates its identifications in strategies of subversion that turn the gaze of the discriminated back upon the eye of power. For the colonial hybrid is the articulation of the ambivalent space where the rite of power is enacted on the site of desire, making its objects at once disciplinary and disseminatory – or, in my mixed metaphor, a negative transparency. (Bhabha, "Signs Taken for Wonders" 154)

Hybridity, thus, is the ontological opposite of transparency, a process of bastardisation that produces a polyphony of identities in contact zones at the level of language – Rushdie describes linguistic hybridity as a process of *chutnification* – race and culture. It may be examined as an enactment of deconstruction, an epistemic and hermeneutic process that does not destroy but rather produces a plurality of meanings. As articulations of ambivalence and heteroglossia, mimicry and hybridity generate each other in a loop of repetitions and subversions. Such a loop is structurally as well as ontologically similar to postmodernist parody and irony that are designed to deconstruct dualisms and the hegemonic discourses that have historically informed narratives of power, production and knowledge.

As Linda Hutcheon argues, perhaps the single most heavily examined interface between the postmodern and the postcolonial, one that has most frequently been visited by critics and theorists alike, is *magic realism*, that liminal conflation of the real and unreal orders marked by a narrative style at once incomplete and excessive. Magic realism, as the stylised rewriting of classic realism and the European and Eurocentric narratives of imperialism and inquest, is characterised by a subversion of the standard notions of space and time and emerges as the site where the postmodern and the postcolonial converge as well as generate new orders of representation. Thus, unsurprisingly, magic realism becomes, as Bhabha describes, "the literary language of the emergent postcolonial world" (*Nation and Narration* 7) with its implicit and sometimes explicit critique of the Western metaphysics of reason. Hutcheon's study of this convergence is interesting. Examining the historicity of the interface between the two "posts", she states,

> At this thematic and structural level, it is not just the relation to history that brings the two *posts* together; there is also a strong shared concern with the notion of marginalization, with the state of what we could call ex-centricity. In granting value to (what the centre calls) the margin or the Other, the postmodern challenges any hegemonic force that presumes centrality, even as it acknowledges that it cannot privilege the margin without acknowledging the power of the centre. ("Circling the Downspout of Empire" 132, italics in original)

Through its entanglement of the representable as well as the unrepresentable, magic realism emerges as an act of writing back as well as forging a new identity and order of articulation.

Akin to postcolonial mimicry as examined by Bhabha, magic realism operates in an economy of hypermimesis and slippery signification, whereby the relationship between the signifier and the signified is permanently problematised and unsettled. As a vehicle for defamiliarisation and departure, magic realism often relies on irony as a subversive tool, another instance of the interface between postmodernism and postcolonial studies. Hutcheon puts this presciently:

> . . . as a double-talking, forked-tongued mode of address, irony becomes a popular rhetorical strategy for working within existing discourses and contesting them at the same time. Its inherent semantic and structural doubleness also makes it a most convenient trope for the paradoxical dualities of both post-modern complicitous critique and post-colonial doubled identity and history. And indeed irony . . . has become a powerful subversive tool in the re-thinking and re-addressing of history by both post-modern and post-colonial artists. ("Circling the Downspout of Empire" 133)

As an act of doubleness as well as disruption, irony, like mimicry and performativity, emerges as a strategy for subversion in postmodern and postcolonial discourses alike. Thus, it becomes a potent tool in the narratives of writers such as Gabriel García Márquez and Salman Rushdie who inhabit the interface between postmodernism and postcolonial writing. Problematising the classic realist tradition that had historically informed the European novel since *Robinson Crusoe*, magic realism is marked by liminality as well as by excess, by epistemic extension as well as interruption, emerging as a critique of Eurocentric ethnography while also being curiously complicit with the cosmopolitanism of the postcolonial world (Aldea 103–10). Magic realism achieves this by bringing "the transcendent and the real together in a hybrid co-presence" and by weaving within "its field of representation phenomena and feelings that lie beyond the grasp of mimetic representation" (Sasser 211).

The entanglement of mimicry, hybridity and ironic identities is perhaps best manifested in real social situations that showcase colonial, postcolonial and postmodern productions of spaces and selves, in sites that have been famously classified by Mary Louise Pratt as *contact zones*. Describing the discursive and embodied interactions characterising such spaces, Pratt points out how the same are informed by structures of sly civility, misappropriations and excess. Thus, she defines contact zones as "social spaces where cultures meet, clash, and grapple with each other, often in contexts of highly asymmetrical relations of power, such as colonialism, slavery, or their aftermaths as they are lived out in many parts of the world today" ("Arts of the Contact Zone" 34). Pratt's definition of the contact zone as the interstitial site for embodied and epistemic exchanges is reflective of a reality determined by disruptions and appearances where autoethnographic texts are "merged or infiltrated to varying degrees with indigenous idioms to create self-representations intended to intervene in metropolitan modes of understanding" ("Arts of the Contact Zone" 35). More significantly, contact zones as described by Pratt offer a direct understanding of the liminality informing the production and performance of postcolonial as well as postmodern identities. The postmodern metropolis may often bear structural and functional parallels with the postcolonial contact zone with its architectural, linguistic and ethnic hybridity as the site of velocity, violence and epistemic exchange "where the physical will of the city, the ego fevers, the assertions of industry, commerce and crowds shape every anecdotal moment"(DeLillo 41).

It is interesting to observe how the politics of praxis in the contact zone – a mutable map marked by identity-switching and hyperlinked narratives – corresponds closely to a postmodern condition marked by mimicry and plasticity that are designed to destabilise any ontology of origin and any metaphysics of essence. Thus, Pratt's idea of the postcolonial contact zone bears remarkable resemblance to Edward Soja's notion of the *postmetropolis* that historically emerged with "[p]ostfordist economic restructuring, intensified globalization, the communication and information revolution, the deterritorialization and reterritorialization of cultures and identity" that are linked to "our mental or cognitive mappings of urban reality and the interpretive grids through which we think about, experience, evaluate and decide to act in the places, spaces, and communities in which we live" (324).

Contact zones emerge, as Pratt would go on to describe in a later work, as sites of self-fashioning where the play between the self and the other is almost always marked by memories and fantasies. In her work, Pratt chooses Gabriel García Márquez's *One Hundred Years of Solitude* (1967) in order to describe the randomness of reception and reproduction that characterise the colonial as well as the neocolonial contact zone marked by memories of loss and wish fulfillment. Pratt describes Macondo, the fictional and fantastic city in Márquez's novel, thus:

> From the opening encounter with the mysterious block of ice brought by the gypsies, Macondo is brought into being as a destination and a receptor. History and time are there marked by uncontrollable, unpredictable arrivals of people, things, institutions and meanings from elsewhere. The inhabitants absorb, examine, adjust, accept, adapt, invent, enjoy, administer, knowing nothing about where things come from or how they originated. . . . In Macondo modernity arrives magically but neocolonially, unsolicited and in bits and pieces – the player piano, the railroad, the banana company. It becomes the raw materials with which the characters, like the novelist himself, negotiate, interact and create. (*Imperial Eyes* 227)

The description of the hybrid, interstitial and liminal contact zone in magic realist fiction foregrounds the close alliance between postmodern and postcolonial politics of representation where magical and metropolitan orders coexist through asymmetrical absorption, assimilation and revisions. As a bazaar of bastardisation and pseudo-production, Macondo in Márquez's novel emerges as a postcolonial as well as postmodern contact zone where modernity is almost always an unfinished project. The rest of the chapter will examine this entanglement and the miscegenation characterising postmodernist as well as postcolonial representations with a study of selected texts.

Hari Kunzru's 2002 debut novel titled *The Impressionist* is a good example of the alliance between postmodernism and postcolonialism in terms of the conflation of identities, where the protagonist Pran is essentially irrecoverable as a stable self from the crowd of postcolonial and postmodern identities he has conferred upon himself through his life and activities. Like Kipling's Kim, whose Irish protagonist presents a playfully ludic self with his fluency in "Hindustani" (an anglicised classification of Hindi and its family of North Indian languages) and familiarity with North Indian landscapes, Kunzru's protagonist too is a hyphenated identity in terms of physiognomy, culture and language, being the fruit of an amorous affair between a colonial British tea planter and an Indian money lender's daughter. Brought up in a Brahmin household in colonial Agra, mistakenly believed to be the biological son of the house pandit and subsequently thrown out with the knowledge of his illegitimacy, Pran in Kunzru's novel variously embodies a woman named Rukhsana in a hermaphrodite's brothel, a white boy named Bobby and finally a gentleman named Jonathan Bridgeman, thus directly performing racial as well as gender hybridity that is postcolonial as well as postmodern in its foregrounding of the liminal quality that informs his miscegenation and personal fantasies. As an entanglement of the postmodern and postcolonial aesthetics of representation,

Kunzru's *The Impressionist* presents a "polyphonic text that employs many different narrative tones – ribald, tender, impressionistic, satirical and fantastical – and that strategically deploys direct intertexts to form the fabric of the picaresque tale" (Morey 86).

The interstitiality characterising the existential and cognitive condition overdetermining the protagonist Pran's condition is described in the novel by the character inhabiting "the limit of perception, materializing . . . like someone only semi-real" (Kunzru 237). If the liminality informing Pran's character and life narrative testifies how his state of being is almost always a state of becoming, it also demonstrates how such condition eschews any easy alliance with reality. This "semi-real" interstitiality unsurprisingly extends onto a political condition whereby the racial identity of Pran is described as "white, yet not white" (234). The hyphenated and performative identities in Kunzru's novel are further problematised by the protagonist's travels across various personal and political spaces, from post–Jallianwala Bagh-massacre-Amritsar (where he is mistaken as a white boy by Indians and British officers alike) to imperial Britain where the miscegenated Pran travels in order to become the perfect British gentleman, the identity that unsurprisingly contains the highest prestige quotient for him.

Like Bhabha's discourse on the negative transparency informing the threshold-quality of mimicry, the interstitial identity-formations determining Kunzru's protagonist are foregrounded by their superficial ontologisation. This is described in the section where Pran fashions himself as the white boy Bobby:

> Bobby is a creature of surface. . . . He hints at transparency. . . . Maybe, instead of imagining depth, all the people who do not quite know him should accept that Bobby's skin is not a boundary between things but the thing itself, a screen on which certain effects take place. Ephemeral curiosities. Tricks of the light. (65)

The tricks of the light and the play of surfaces as opposed to depth reveal a postmodern break from any ontology of origin or metaphysics of essence that inform humanist understandings of identity. Instead what is described is an endless entanglement of surfaces whereby the key to identity rests not in the stable self but in the performative one. More significantly, as the passage above makes clear, the threshold of Bobby's skin is not a passageway to hidden depths or meanings but is the floating signifier of meaning itself, enacting a play between white and non-white identities. As a "creature of surface", and as an incomplete hybrid between coloniser and colonised identities, Bobby embodies postcolonial as well as postmodern attributes. Ending with a spectacle of bewilderment in the African wilderness whereby the protagonist's constructed categories of identity dissolve away, *The Impressionist* makes ample intertextual references to Kipling's *Kim* (1901) with Pran grappling for directions geographically as well as existentially: "For now the journey is everything. He has no thoughts of arriving anywhere. Tonight he will sleep under the enormous bowl of the sky. Tomorrow he will travel on" (465).

If Kunzru's novel is set in imperial India and presents a protagonist who is polyphonic and hybridised in terms of biological, cultural and linguistic identities, it also shows how the same protagonist aspires for and attempts to achieve the hegemonic white British masculinity through a process of appropriation. In contrast, Gautam Malkani's 2006 debut novel *Londonstani* presents a picture of youth subcultures in Hounslow right before the 2005 London bombings and proffers a play of identities in a postcolonial postmodern metropolis whose messy multiculturalism eschews any special privileging of white racial identity. As a newly joined member of the Punjabi gang in Hounslow, Jas, the protagonist in Malkani's novel, embodies the contingent racial identity in post-imperial Britain where consumerism and commodification supplant ideological alliance and brave new causes. Malkani's novel is refreshingly radical in its reversal of the normative direction of mimicry as it presents a protagonist who aspires to appropriate the *desi* idiom in Britain while being racially and ethnically white.

The very title of Malkani's novel is reflective of the complex contact zone that is twenty-first-century Britain where racial miscegenation and linguistic hybridity problematise any easy equation between postcolonialism and multiculturalism (Gunew 22–39). In its dramatic dissemination of inconstant identities where racial profiling is problematised by complex aspirations, Malkani's novel offers an entanglement of the postcolonial and postmodern orders of representation. It does so with graphic and realistic descriptions of countercultural boy gangs in twenty-first-century Britain and how the hegemonic homosociality in the same is premised on performative masculinity and mimicry of the "desi cool" which emerges as a resistance against white privilege in the postmodern post-imperial urban space. *Londonstani* opens with a white boy being beaten up for calling someone a "Paki", in a curious reversal of Paki-bashing prevalent in the 1960s. The narrator Jas – one who aspires to fit into the cool desi gang despite his white ethnicity which is revealed in the end – hastens to describe the complex identity politics in the racially complex boy gang: "First we was rudeboys, then we be Indian niggas, then rajamuffins, then raggastanis, Britasians, fuckin Indobrits. These days we try an use our own word for homeboy an so we just call ourselves desis" (6).

The markers of identity used in the description above reveal a complex conflation of Asian, Caribbean and imperial ethnic backgrounds through historical processes of miscegenation and hybridity. Thus, "rudeboys", historically used to describe settlers in Britain who were of African origin and could not be racially bullied by the whites, was quickly replaced by "Indian niggas" and then "rajamuffins", a term pejoratively used to describe non-white settlers from the erstwhile space of the Raj. The movement of identity markers to describe non-whiteness also reveals an ambivalent shift from problem to privilege as "desi" comes to suggest a new performative order of urban male identity in a postmodern, post-imperial ethnography. The desi identity as described in Malkani's *Londonstani* is a complex of *postmodern cool* and postcolonial resentment with its economy of anxieties and structures of resistance. Thus, Hardjit, the alpha male leader of the desi gang, confesses that he does not want to end up "workin in Heathrow fuckin airport helping goras catch planes to places so they could turn their own skin brown" (23). The domestic desi thus articulates his difference as well as his ambivalent location between inferiority and privilege apropos of the wealthy white in a postcolonial asymmetrically multicultural Britain.

The postcolonial presence in Malkani's *Londonstani* is complemented and corroborated by the postmodern idiom it appropriates which dramatises a play between the real and the virtual in intimate as well as in homosocial spaces. This is stylistically supplemented by the presence of an unreliable trickster narrator (we find out right in the end that Jas is far from being naturally desi and that he is, in fact, white) and by intertextual allusions, not least to the Wachowskis' 1999 film *The Matrix*, itself a cult-work in postmodern aesthetics (Malkani 238). In its mosaic of heteroglossia (a carnivalesque construct of Caribbean, Punjabi and British slangs) and slippery axes of signification and representation, Malkani's *Londonstani* is an excellent example of postcolonial abrogation as well as Mikhail Bakhtin's notion of the artistic image of language as a linguistic and intentional hybrid where the entanglement of two orders of consciousness – the one being represented and the other doing the representing – manage to penetrate the interiority of speech and establish a performative, perspectival quality (Bakhtin, "Discourse in the Novel" 358–59). The classic postmodern rejection of essence and approximation of the immediate is revealed in "Rudeboy Rule # 4" in Malkani's novel which describes the coded quality in the constructed homosociality of the desi boy gang, as the narrator Jas states how "[a]ccording to Hardjit, it don't matter if the proper word for something sounds fuckin ridiculous. If it's the proper word then it's the proper word" (45). Jas's struggle to appropriate the subculture dialect is described at the very beginning of the novel:

> . . . I still can't attain the right level a rudeboy finesse. If I could, I wouldn't be using poncey words like attain an finesse, innit. I'd be saying I couldn't keep it real or someshit. An if I said it that way, then there'd be no need for me to say it in the first place so I wouldn't say it anyway. After all, it's all about what you say an how you say it. (6)

An excellent example of the entanglement between the postcolonial and the postmodern world orders features in Malkani's novel as the narrator Jas describes the caste system as an invented category for social stratification, linking it further with the virtual world of illusions in *The Matrix*:

> – No, my friend, I go, – castes don't exist. It's all bullshit, all in *The Matrix*, all part a some illusion created by people who want power over others. You did history with Mr Ashwood, right? The world's full a categories a people that were just, like, invented randomly. How can someone be Brahmin and someone not be Brahmin if the categories don't really exist in the real world? (239)

The scene here features a character named Arun and his anxiety about his fiancé Reena's non-brahmannical status that upsets his mother. Jas's denunciation of established rules – describing the act of doing something just because it's tradition as "a lame excuse for not havin a proper reason" (237) – incorporates postcolonial rejection as well as postmodern skepticism. Mr Ashwood, the school teacher in the novel, is an embodiment of old-school Englishness as well as the mouthpiece of radical thought in an interesting complex of conservatism and skepticism in *Londonstani*. With its inconstant allusions to popular culture, contemporary politics and deconstructions of racialised presuppositions, Malkani's novel is a tour de force of postmodernist storytelling where embodied identities are extended by consumed identities that operate by appropriations, illusions and deceptions. In a complex of the postcolonial and postmodern orders of representation, *Londonstani* reveals how hybridity itself emerges as a commodity in a multicultural world. Thus, Sanjay in Malkani's novel aims to invest in a chef who "fuses Japanese, Lebanese and traditional kosher food" as his research reveals that "it's the only fusion experience that the London scene doesn't offer yet" (161).

At the end of the novel, when it is revealed to the reader that Jas is, in fact, a white boy who had been mimicking the desi discourse throughout the novel, the earlier allusions return with renewed irony. Thus, the comparison of Jas's physiognomic features with that of Justin Timberlake becomes a double irony of sorts: a white boy who aspires to be a part of the non-white, cool, desi boy gang compared to a white musician who appropriates a musical genre pioneered by Black artists. The performative mimicry in *Londonstani* thus inhabits the interface between postcolonial and postmodern politics of representation and embodiment. If Jas's appropriation of desi subculture may be read as an optimistic example of interracial mobility in a multicultural Britain, the novel's innately postmodernist indeterminacy also ensures that the reader is unsure about the stage of such integration or about the desirability of the same in a post-imperial contact zone (Perfect 151). This postmodern, postcolonial uncertainty about the ontology of multicultural integration is embedded throughout the narrative of *Londonstani* – dramatised at the end by the revelation of the narrator's white ethnicity – and allows the narrative to examine the fault lines that accompany identity-formations in a world where a person can become someone else as quickly as unblocking a mobile phone and be "given a new identity" (Malkani 71).

The play of irony, mimicry and performed identities is dramatised in Caryl Phillips's 2006 novel *Dancing in the Dark* that retells the life narrative of Bert Williams, the first Black entertainer in Broadway, who had to embody, enact and extend his racial stereotype on stage for it to be consumed by a paying audience. Williams in Phillips's novel darkens his face with burnt cork and performs as a dim-witted Black man in complete compliance with the racial performance expected of him. In a spectacular testimony to the ambivalence of mimicry as described by Bhabha, the protagonist of Phillips's novel contemplates,

> No longer Egbert Austin Williams. He kept telling himself, I am no longer Egbert Austin Williams. As I apply the burnt cork to my face, as I smear the black into my already sable skin, as I put on my lips, I am leaving behind Egbert Austin Williams. However, I can, at any time, reclaim this man with soap and water and the rugged application of a coarse towel. (57)

The passage reveals the contingent production of mimicry whereby the performed identity ceases to be separable from the performing self in a cognitive condition that bears interesting parallels with the postmodern blurring of borderlines between the real and the virtual.

Williams in Phillips's novel comes to the realisation that the ontic self is not recoverable from the plastic performative one in a consumerist culture where race and identity emerge as malleable acts of appropriation rather than stable entities. The instability of identities is reflected by the fragmented form in *Dancing in the Dark* that weaves in a plurality of perspectives, non-fictional passages and narrative voices, including those of Walker's, Williams's, Lottie's, a fragment from a 1910 New York Age article and a third-person narrator. As Abigail Ward states, "[t]he reader is expected not so much to straightforwardly piece together these narratives into a whole, but rather to recognise that there is no 'true' narrative regarding Williams: he is both traitor and advancer of the 'Negro race'; fool and genius" (107). The ambivalent position of Williams the performer as a fool as well as genius bears testimony to the postmodern production of interstitial identities whereby race and racial classifications are consumed in their performative states, much like the postmodern productions of gender and gendered identities as examined in the previous chapter.

The postcolonial turn has historically been quite synchronous with that of the postmodern one, with the major Asian and African colonies controlled by European nations beginning to attain their independence after the Second World War, which may also be classified as the era that marks the beginning of postmodernism as indicated in the chronology offered at the end of this book. As Kimberly Chabot Davis argues, to accuse postmodernism of embedded Eurocentricity is to miss the complex engagement postmodernism has historically had with Black movements, feminism and gender studies. Thus, "[a]ny claim that the lives of black people have nothing to do with postmodernism ignores the complex historical interrelationship of black protest and liberal academic discourse. . . . racial liberation movements of the 1960s and 70s (as well as the feminist movement) contributed to the loosening of cultural boundaries, a change that is seen as characteristically postmodern" (Davis 244).[1] Identity is indeed a crucial category in postmodernism and postcolonialism where the play between binaries and boundaries emerges not as a destruction of locations but a freeing up of the same, informing as well as being informed by performativity, hybridity and mimicry. The alliances between postmodernism and postcolonialism incorporate an interest in irony, the fictionality of history and a strategic "attentiveness to fragmentation and the gaps and silences within the archive" (Ward 100). As this chapter attempted to examine, the postmodern postcolonial, far from being a contradiction in terms, offers a complex and comprehensive area of enquiry that problematises popularly received notions of race, space, gender and identity, often with active interventions enacted by technology, language and the body. Such enquiry is increasingly relevant in the glocalised world orders where cultures of consumption and cultures of belonging are often simultaneously irreconcilable and indistinguishable (Roudometof 101).

Works Cited

Aldea, Eva. *Magical Realism and Deleuze: The Indiscernibility of Difference in Postcolonial Literature*. London: Continuum, 2011. Print.

Ashcroft, Bill. "Critical Histories: Postcolonialism, Postmodernism and Race." *Postmodern Literature and Race*. Ed. Len Platt and Sara Upstone. Cambridge: Cambridge UP, 2015. 13–20. Print.

Appiah, Kwame Anthony. "Is the Post- in Postmodernism the Post- in Postcolonial?" *Critical Inquiry* 17.2 (1991): 336–57. Print.

Bakhtin, Mikhail. "Discourse in the Novel." *The Dialogic Imagination*. Ed. Michael Holquist. Trans. Caryl Emerson and Michael Holquist. Austin, TX: U of Texas P, 1981. 259–422. Print.

---. *The Dialogic Imagination: Four Essays*. Ed. Michael Holquist. Trans. Caryl Emerson and Michael Holquist. Austin, TX: U of Texas P, 1981. Print.

Bhabha, Homi K. *Nation and Narration*. London: Psychology Press, 1990. Print.

---. "Of Mimicry and Man: The Ambivalence of Colonial Discourse." *October* 28 (1984): 125–33. Print.

---. "Signs Taken for Wonders: Questions of Ambivalence and Authority under a Tree outside Delhi, May 1817." *Critical Inquiry* 12.1 (1985): 144–65. Print.

---. *The Location of Culture*. London: Routledge, 1994. Print.

Chakrabarty, Dipesh. *Provincializing Europe: Postcolonial Thought and Historical Difference*. Princeton, NJ: Princeton UP, 2000. Print.

Davis, Kimberly Chabot. "'Postmodern Blackness': Toni Morrison's *Beloved* and the End of History." *Twentieth Century Literature* 44.2 (1998): 242–60. Print.

DeLillo, Don. *Cosmopolis.* New York: Scribner, 2003. Print.

Gunew, Sneja. "Postcolonialism and Multiculturalism: Between Race and Ethnicity." *The Yearbook of English Studies* 27 (1997): 22–39. Print.

Hoesterey, Ingeborg. *Pastiche: Cultural Memory in Art, Film, Literature.* Bloomington and Indianapolis: Indiana UP, 2001. Print.

Hutcheon, Linda. "'Circling the Downspout of Empire': Post-Colonialism and Postmodernism." *Ariel* 20.4 (1989): 149–75. Print.

---. *Narcissistic Narrative: The Metafictional Paradox.* Waterloo, Ontario: Wilfrid Laurier UP, 1980. Print.

Kunzru, Hari. *The Impressionist.* London: Penguin, 2003. Print.

Malkani, Gautam. *Londonstani.* London: Fourth Estate, 2006. Print.

Monteiro-Ferreira, Ana. "Afrocentricity and the Western Paradigm." *Journal of Black Studies* 40.2 (2009): 327–36. Print.

Morey, Peter. "Performing Identity: Intertextuality, Race and Difference in the South Asian Novel in English." *Postmodern Literature and Race.* Ed. Len Platt and Sarah Upstone. New York: Cambridge UP, 2015. 82–97. Print.

Nandy, Ashis. "History's Forgotten Doubles." *History and Theory* 34 (1995): 44–46. Print.

Perfect, Michael. *Contemporary Fictions of Multiculturalism: Diversity and the Millennial London Novel.* London: Palgrave Macmillan, 2014. Print.

Phillips, Caryl. *Dancing in the Dark.* London: Vintage, 2006. Print.

Pratt, Mary Louise. "Arts of the Contact Zone." *Profession* (1991): 33–40. Print.

---. *Imperial Eyes: Travel Writing and Transculturation.* New York: Routledge, 2008. Print.

Roudometof, Victor. *Glocalization: A Critical Introduction.* New York: Routledge, 2016. Print.

Rushdie, Salman. *Shame*. New York: Random House, 2008. Print.

Sasser, Kim Anderson. *Magical Realism and Cosmopolitanism: Strategizing Belonging*. New York: Palgrave Macmillan, 2014. Print.

Soja, Edward. *Postmetropolis: Critical Studies of Cities and Regions*. Malden, MA: Blackwell, 2000. Print.

Ward, Abigail. "Performing Race in Caryl Phillips's *Dancing in the Dark*." *Postmodern Literature and Race*. Ed. Len Platt and Sara Upstone. Cambridge: Cambridge UP, 2015. 98–112. Print.

Warnes, Christopher. *Magical Realism and the Postcolonial Novel: Between Faith and Irreverence*. New York: Palgrave Macmillan, 2009. Print.

Notes

1. Likewise, Ana Monteiro-Ferreira argues in favour of the usefulness of the postmodernist perspective in a study of African-American works (332).

Conclusion

Samuel Beckett's *Endgame* begins with the character Clov pronouncing: "Finished, it's finished, nearly finished, it must be nearly finished" (93). Looking back from 2018, one is tempted to speak of postmodernism in similar terms, as a project that must nearly be finished. However, Beckett's line in itself contains the productive paradox that underpins much of postmodernist poetics. It is a project that is *almost always nearly finished* and unlike the unfinished project of modernity described by Jürgen Habermas, the unfinished project of postmodernism is not in opposition to its ontological extension but rather emerges as an affirmation of it. For postmodernism is nothing if not an unfinished Beckettian play, forever marked by interstices and interruptions that espouse reversals instead of closures, cyclicality instead of linearity, with a disregard for any metaphysical metanarrative of meaningful productivity and closure. Postmodernist poetics frequently shuns any neat sense of beginning, middle and end, and frequently defies the logic of spatiality and temporality. Postmodernism eschews any eschatological understanding of the world and relies instead on the immediately local and textual. It is often produced by contested and contesting categories of knowledge, seldom aiming for a sense of an ending. In a postmodernist sense, postmodernism is perhaps almost always ending; will perhaps never fully end.

This book has made an attempt to trace the trajectory and various narratives of postmodernism through a study of selected literary texts. It has examined postmodernism's entanglements with history, technology, gender and race, among other issues, while also attempting to describe some of the key features recurrent in postmodernist poetics. Special attention has thus been given to the metafictional, intertextual and heteroglossic qualities of postmodernist texts that offer a complex interplay of real and virtual identities, sometimes further problematised by irony and performativity. This book has also attempted to explore the self-consciousness that informs postmodernist descriptions of noise and nonsense that inconsistently unsettle meaningful sounds and metanarratives of meanings. The same self-consciousness also informs the ontology of unreliability in postmodernist fiction that often operates through characterisations and narrative strategies.

Exploring the areas between sex and gender, body and appearance, ethnicity and identity, and organicity and artificiality, postmodernism and postmodernist fiction have often generated new orders of representation and understanding that are inexhaustible precisely because of their non-dualistic ontology. This book has attempted to examine the postmodernist incredulity towards dualistic metanarratives through a study of selected texts that are deliberately unreliable, incomplete and inconsistently subversive. The incompletion and incorporation of losses and lacks form a part of postmodernist poetics, in contrast to the nostalgia for lost unity and harmony characterising modernism. As Andreas Huyssen puts it,

> Just as Marx analyzed the culture of modernity dialectically as bringing both progress and destruction, the culture of postmodernity, too, must be grasped in its gains as well as in its losses, in its promises as well as in its depravations; and yet, it may be precisely one of the characteristics of the postmodern that the relationship between progress and destruction of cultural forms, between tradition and modernity can no longer be understood today the same way Marx understood it at the dawn of modernist culture. (29–30)

This book has tried to examine the ontological complexity as well as the attitudinal ambivalence characterising the postmodern perspective, one that rejects any unequivocal binary of progress and loss, production and parody. Emerging, as Zygmunt Bauman argues, as "modernity without illusions", the poetics of postmodernity is perhaps best suited to examining the "messy and ambiguous" quality of human reality (32).

Finally, this book has also attempted to unpack the historicity and historical awareness of postmodernism and postmodernist literature that often emerge as a deconstruction and debunking of hegemonic history and a production of alternative historical orders. Far from being insensitive to history and being characterised by "anything goes", postmodernism and postmodernist literature are marked by several stylistic and thematic categories that capture the constructed qualities of history and historical knowledge that often operate as coercive apparatus in discourse networks. Perhaps the greatest gift of postmodernism is a systematic study of constructedness and discursivity disguised as metadiscursive givens and a subsequent celebration of cynicism and certaintylessness. This is done with unreliable narratives, trickster narrators and ludic turns that debunk the myth of chronological closures while simultaneously deconstructing the normativity informing shared understandings of sexuality, body and identity. It is thus unsurprising, as this book has hopefully managed to examine, that postmodernism has found its ideological allies in feminism, postcolonialism and posthumanism in their shared suspicion of any metaphysics of essence. With its celebration of simulation, promotion of textuality and alliance with interstitiality, postmodernist literature has been a potent tool to unsettle the archaeology of authority and knowledge that had historically and discursively informed ideas of supremacy at political as well as epistemic levels. With its self-reflexivity and certaintylessness, its extended worlds and immersive interiority, postmodernism offers "the possibility of a radically novel understanding of moral phenomena" in its scope and function (Bauman 3). Its increasing significance in the real and virtual worlds we inhabit today can hardly be overestimated.

Works Cited

Bauman, Zygmunt. *Postmodern Ethics*. Oxford and Cambridge, MA: Blackwell, 1993. Print.

Beckett, Samuel. *Endgame. The Complete Dramatic Works*. London: Faber and Faber, 1986. 89–134. Print.

Habermas, Jürgen. *The Philosophical Discourse of Modernity: Twelve Lectures*. Trans. Frederick Lawrence. Cambridge, MA: MIT Press, 1987. Print.

Huyssen, Andreas. "Mapping the Postmodern." *New German Critique* 33 (Autumn 1984): 5–52. Print.

Timeline

Events	Important Publications
1939: Arnold Toynbee first uses the term *postmodern* in volume 5 of *A Study of History*	Jorge Luis Borges, "Pierre Menard, autor del Quijote", *Sur* (first short story)
The Irish Republican Army (IRA) begins a bombing campaign in Britain	James Joyce, *Finnegans Wake* (last work)
	Batman Comics released
First nuclear fission experiment in Columbia University	John Steinbeck, *Grapes of Wrath*
Adolf Hitler invades Czechoslovakia	Flann O'Brien, *At Swim-Two-Birds*
Sigmund Freud dies	W. H. Auden, "September 1, 1939"
W. B. Yeats dies	
Beginning of the Second World War	
Jean-Paul Sartre is conscripted in the French Army as a meteorologist	
1941: James Joyce dies	
Rabindranath Tagore dies	
Henri Bergson dies	
Virginia Woolf commits suicide	
Marina Tsvetaeva commits suicide	
Bertolt Brecht's *Mother Courage and Her Children* first performed in Switzerland	
Orson Welles's *Citizen Kane* released in the US	

1945: Premiere of Tennessee Williams's *The Glass Menagerie* Nazi Party newspaper *Völkischer Beobachter* ceases publication Adolf Hitler commits suicide US drops atomic bombs at Hiroshima and Nagasaki End of Second World War United Nations formed	George Orwell, *Animal Farm*
1947: India gains independence Geoffrey Kendal arrives in India with his theatre troupe *Shakespeareana* Tennessee Williams's *A Streetcar Named Desire* opens at Broadway directed by Elia Kazan starring Jessica Tandy and Marlon Brando	Thomas Mann, *Doctor Faustus* Albert Camus, *The Plague* Gabriel García Márquez, *Eyes of a Blue Dog* (first short story collection)
1948: First colour newsreel filmed by Warner Brothers Assassination of Mahatma Gandhi Bertolt Brecht's *The Caucasian Chalk Circle* first performed Wireway develops the first magnetic tape recorder First flight of a radio-controlled airplane First newsreel telecast "20th Century Fox-Movietone News"	Thornton Wilder, *The Ides of March* G. V. Desani, *All about H. Hatterr*
1949: First photo of the gene taken by Daniel Pease Richard Baker	George Orwell, *Nineteen Eighty-Four*

Premiere of Arthur Miller's *Death of a Salesman* in New York	Simone de Beauvoir, *The Second Sex*
First atomic energy museum opens at Oak Ridge	First magazine on microfilm, *Newsweek*, published
Communists in India arrested en masse	
Albert Camus's *The Just Assassins* premieres in Paris	
First woman ambassador, Vijaya Lakshmi Pandit from India, received in the US	
1951: Ludwig Wittgenstein dies	J. D. Salinger, *The Catcher in the Rye*
First Berlin International Film Festival	Albert Camus, *The Rebel*
First Commercial Computer UNIVAC 1 appears	Nirad C. Chaudhuri, *The Autobiography of an Unknown Indian*
	Vladimir Nabokov, *Speak, Memory* (autobiography)
1953: Queen Elizabeth II crowned as the sovereign of United Kingdom, Australia, Canada, New Zealand, South Africa, Pakistan and Ceylon	Roland Barthes, *Writing Degree Zero*
Samuel Beckett's *En attendant Godot* (*Waiting for Godot*) premieres in Paris	
Premiere of *Adventures of Superman* TV series	
Joseph Stalin dies	
First 3D TV broadcast experiment in the US	

1954: Akira Kurosawa's *Seven Samurai* released

The National Negro Network appears in the US with 40 radio stations

Elvis Presley records his first songs in a Memphis studio

First shopping mall opens in Michigan

Premiere of Walt Disney's first TV show "Disneyland"

First celebration of Bloomsday takes place in Dublin, organised by Flann O'Brien, Patrick Kavanagh and Anthony Cronin

Kingsley Amis, *Lucky Jim*

William Golding, *Lord of the Flies*

1954–62: Algerian War of Independence

1955: Albert Einstein dies

Thomas Mann dies

Satyajit Ray's *Pather Panchali* (Song of the Road) released

Waiting for Godot first performed in English

Beginning of the Vietnam War

Vladimir Nabokov, *Lolita*

Saadat Hasan Manto, "Toba Tek Singh"

1956: England intervenes in the Suez Canal crisis, withdraws after US pressure

John Osborne's *Look Back in Anger* first performed, heralding the Angry Young Men movement in theatre

First issue of *The Ladder*, the first lesbian magazine in the US, published

Norman Mailer, *The White Negro*

Allen Ginsberg, *Howl and Other Poems*

Elvis Presley releases his eponymous debut album
Bertolt Brecht dies

Saul Bellow, *Seize the Day*
Khushwant Singh, *Train to Pakistan*

1957: Launch of *Sputnik* satellite by USSR
Samuel Beckett's *Endgame* first performed

Isaac Asimov, *Earth is Room Enough*, *The Naked Sun*
John Braine, *Room at the Top*
Jack Kerouac, *On the Road*
Jean-Paul Sartre, *Existentialism and Human Emotions*
Roland Barthes, *Mythologies*

1958: Discovery of DNA
First march against nuclear tests in Aldermaston, Britain
French settlers in Algeria start riot against the stationed French army
Cuban President Batista begins battle against the revolutionary army of Fidel Castro
Emergency declared in Algeria
Harold Pinter's *The Birthday Party* premieres
Samuel Beckett's *Krapp's Last Tape* premieres

Chinua Achebe, *Things Fall Apart*

1959: Fidel Castro becomes Prime Minister of Cuba after the overthrow of the Batista regime
C. P. Snow delivers the Rede Lecture entitled "The Two Cultures" at the Senate House, Cambridge, an event that would subsequently spark the famous

Asterix the Gaul first appears in the comic magazine *Pilote*
Günter Grass, *The Tin Drum*

"Two Cultures Debate" between Snow and F. R. Leavis François Truffaut's *Les Quatre cents coups* (*The 400 Blows*) released	
1960: Cameroon gains independence from France Albert Camus dies in a car accident Jean-Luc Godard's *À bout de souffle (Breathless)* released, marking the beginning of French New Wave cinema D. H. Lawrence's *Lady Chatterley's Lover* judged not obscene by US Supreme Court	First issue of *Tel Quel* journal published
1961: Berlin Wall created Ernest Hemingway commits suicide	Joseph Heller, *Catch-22* V. S. Naipaul, *A House for Mr. Biswas* R. K. Narayan, *The Man-Eater of Malgudi*
1962: *Space War*, the first computer game, begins to circulate	
1963: The Beatles release their debut album *Please Please Me* Martin Luther King delivers "I Have a Dream" speech Sylvia Plath commits suicide US President Kennedy assassinated	Thomas Pynchon, *V.* (first novel)

1964: Terry Riley composes *In C*, foundational work of minimalist music

Peter Weiss's *Marat/Sade* performed

Saul Bellow, *Herzog*

Girish Karnad, *Tughlaq*

1965: First spacewalk by Alexey Leonov

Ngũgĩ wa Thiong'o, *The River Between*

Sylvia Plath, *Ariel* (published posthumously)

1966: National Organization for Women founded in the US

Jacques Derrida delivers the lecture "Structure, Sign, and Play in the Discourse of the Human Sciences" at Johns Hopkins University

Samuel Beckett's *Come and Go* first performed

Thomas Pynchon, *The Crying of Lot 49*

Noam Chomsky, *Cartesian Linguistics*

A. K. Ramanujan, *The Striders*

Jean Rhys, *Wide Sargasso Sea*

Jacques Lacan, *Écrits*

1967: Detroit race riots

Six-Day (Arab–Israeli) War

Che Guevara executed

Decriminalisation of homosexuality between male adults in UK

Guy Debord, "The Society of the Spectacle"

Roland Barthes, "The Death of the Author"

Jacques Derrida, *L'écriture et la différence* (*Writing and Difference*, 1978), *La voix et le phénomène* (*Speech and Phenomena*, 1973) and *De la grammatologie* (*Of Grammatology*, 1976)

Gabriel García Márquez, *Cien años de soledad* (*One Hundred Years of Solitude*, 1970)

First issue of *Flash Art* journal published

1968: Nationwide riots and protests in France

USSR invades Czechoslovakia

Stanley Kubrick's *2001: A Space Odyssey* released

Intel Corporations created in the US

Martin Luther King Jr. assassinated

The first interracial kissing scene shown on US TV in *Star Trek*

1969: Neil Armstrong becomes the first person to step on the moon

Establishment of ARPANET (Advanced Research Projects Agency Network), forerunner of the internet, linking together universities of Stanford, UCSB, UCLA, and Utah

Gay Liberation Front established in New York

Jack Kerouac dies

Kurt Vonnegut, *Slaughterhouse-Five*

John Fowles, *The French Lieutenant's Woman*

1970:

Toni Morrison, *The Bluest Eye*

Germaine Greer, *The Female Eunuch*

1971:

Ihab Hassan, *POSTmodernISM: A Paracritical Bibliography*

E. M. Forster, *Maurice* (posthumously published)

Aleksandr Solzhenitsyn, *August 1914*

1972: Demolition of Pruitt-Igoe, failed urban housing project in St Louis	First issue of *boundary 2: an international journal of literature and culture* published
Debut of David Bowie as the androgynous Ziggy Stardust with the single "Starman"	Robert Venturi, Denise Scott Brown and Steven Isenour, *Learning from Las Vegas*
Debut of Michael Jackson as a solo artist with the album *Got to be there*	Noam Chomsky, *Pentagon Papers*
	Italo Calvino, *Invisible Cities*
Samuel Beckett's *Not I* first performed	
1973: Pablo Neruda dies W. H. Auden dies	Thomas Pynchon, *Gravity's Rainbow*
1975: First appearance of the personal computer	E. L. Doctorow, *Ragtime* Carlos Fuentes, *Terra Nostra*
Philip Glass's *Einstein on the Beach* composed	
Hélène Cixous coins the term *Écriture féminine* in her article "Le rire de la Méduse" ("The Laugh of the Medusa")	
The Vietnam War ends	
Arnold Toynbee dies	
1977: Harvey Milk becomes the first openly gay individual elected to public office in California	
1978: The first test-tube baby, Louise Brown, is born in Oldham, England	Edward Said, *Orientalism*
Richard Donner's *Superman* released	

1979: First cellular phone released in Tokyo Jean Rhys dies The Sino-Vietnam war begins Margaret Thatcher becomes the first female Prime Minister of the United Kingdom USSR invades Afghanistan	Jean-François Lyotard, *La condition postmoderne* Italo Calvino, *If on a Winter's Night a Traveller*
1980–81: Jacques Lacan dies MTV launched in New York Richard Serra's *Tilted Arc* appears *The New York Times* reports on appearance of AIDS	Salman Rushdie, *Midnight's Children* Gilles Deleuze and Félix Guattari, *Milles plateau*
1983–84: Michel Foucault dies	Jean Baudrillard, *Simulations* Jean-François Lyotard, *The Postmodern Condition* (English translation of *La condition postmoderne*, 1979) William Gibson, *Neuromancer* Fredric Jameson, *Postmodernism, or, the Cultural Logic of Late Capitalism* Patricia Waugh, *Metafiction*
1985: *Live Aid*, world's first global concert (held simultaneously in London and Philadelphia) Robert Zemeckis's *Back to the Future* released	Donna Haraway, "A Cyborg Manifesto" Don DeLillo, *White Noise*
1986: Wole Soyinka becomes the first black writer to win the Nobel Prize for literature	Kumari Jayawardena, *Feminism and Nationalism in the Third World*

Dennis Potter's *The Singing Detective* broadcast

Simone de Beauvoir dies

Jorge Luis Borges dies

Major nuclear accident takes place at Soviet Union's Chernobyl

1988: Writers Guild of America goes on strike

Noam Chomsky, *Manufacturing Consent: The Political Economy of the Mass Media*

Tsitsi Dangarembga, *Nervous Conditions*

Umberto Eco, *Il pendolo di Foucault (Foucault's Pendulum,* 1989*)*

Salman Rushdie, *Satanic Verses*

1989: Iran's Ayatollah Khomeini issues a fatwa against Salman Rushdie on Valentine's Day

Tiananmen Square protest and massacre in Beijing

Fall of Berlin Wall

Tim Berners-Lee develops the concept of World Wide Web

Francis Fukuyama, "The End of History?"

1990–91: Nelson Mandela released after twenty-seven and a half years of imprisonment

Start of the Persian Gulf War

Reunion of East Germany and West Germany

David Lynch's *Twin Peaks* begins broadcasting

First issue of *Postmodern Culture*, an online journal, published

Judith Butler, *Gender Trouble*

Jean Baudrillard, *The Gulf War did not take place* (published in *Libération* and *The Guardian*)

Martin Amis, *Time's Arrow*

Hitoshi Igarashi, the Japanese translator of Salman Rushdie's *Satanic Verses*, stabbed to death at University of Tsukuba in accordance with the fatwa Rajiv Gandhi assassinated Dissolution of the USSR	
1996: First performance of Eve Ensler's *The Vagina Monologues* Dolly the sheep becomes the first successfully cloned creature	Alan Sokal, "Transgressing the Boundaries: Towards a Transformative Hermeneutics of Quantum Theory" in *Social Text* (hoax essay)
1997: Abbas Kiarostami's *Taste of Cherry* released Allen Ginsberg dies	Arundhati Roy, *The God of Small Things* J. K. Rowling, *Harry Potter and the Philosopher's Stone* (first novel in the Harry Potter series)
1998–99: Jean-François Lyotard dies Peter Weir's *The Truman Show* released Wachowskis' *The Matrix* released	Orhan Pamuk, *My Name is Red* Jhumpa Lahiri, *The Interpreter of Maladies*
2000:	J. K. Rowling, *Harry Potter and the Goblet of Fire*
2001: V. S. Naipaul wins Nobel Prize for literature Al-Qaeda attack destroys World Trade Center in New York on 11 September (9/11)	Salman Rushdie, *Fury* V. S. Naipaul, *Half a Life*
2003: A USA-led coalition invades Iraq	

2009: Carol Ann Duffy becomes the first female and lesbian Poet Laureate of Britain Barack Obama becomes the first black President of the United States of America Britain officially ends military operations in Iraq UNESCO launches the World Digital Library Michael Jackson dies	Carl Jung, *Red Book* (digital version)
2016: Umberto Eco dies David Bowie dies Abbas Kiarostami dies Bob Dylan wins Nobel Prize for literature Britain votes to exit European Union through Brexit polls Donald Trump elected as the 45th President of the United States of America Fidel Castro dies	

Index